THE MANY FACES OF I

THE MANY FACES OF FAITH

*A Guide to World Religions
and Christian Traditions*

Richard R. Losch

William B. Eerdmans Publishing Company
Grand Rapids, Michigan / Cambridge, U.K.

Wm. B. Eerdmans Publishing Co.

255 Jefferson Ave. S.E., Grand Rapids, Michigan 49503 /
P.O. Box 163, Cambridge CB3 9PU U.K.

Printed in the United States of America

05 04 03 02 01   7 6 5 4 3 2 1

Library of Congress Cataloging-in-Publication Data

Losch, Richard R.
The many faces of faith / Richard R. Losch.
p.   cm.
Includes bibliographical references.

ISBN 0-8028-3910-X (alk. paper)
1. Religions. 2. Christian sects. 3. Christianity and
other religions. I. Title.
BL80.2.L67   2001

291 — dc21

2001040274

www.eerdmans.com

Contents

II. THE MANY FACES OF CHRISTIANITY

Preface

In my first year as rector of St. James' Episcopal Church, Livingston, Alabama, I was asked to speak to a local group known as "The Progressive Study Club." Their request was that I speak for about twenty minutes about the various religions of the world. I found the challenge of condensing such a prodigious subject into twenty minutes a bit daunting, but, notwithstanding, I tackled the project. In the process, I discovered how little I really knew about most of the major world religions. I decided to prepare a monthly article for our parish newsletter. When that series was completed, I went on to write about each of the major Christian denominations, and those two series have evolved into this book. It would be a monumental project to write about every single faith and denomination, so I have selected those which seem the most important and influential in the realm of modern human spirituality.

This is not intended to be a scholarly or in-depth work. Rather, it is an attempt to familiarize the reader with the main customs and beliefs of these groups, and to dispel many of the myths and misconceptions that so pervade our common beliefs about them. Those who wish to pursue a deeper understanding of any of these groups are strongly encouraged to do so, and in this age of information there are countless resources available. Web pages about the groups are one important source, although a certain level of discernment must be developed, especially when dealing with unofficial web pages.

I have yet to decide which is more difficult — being objective from within or from outside one's personal experience. It is hard to explain something with which we have had no direct involvement, but it is at least as hard to look at our own experiences and beliefs from the outside. Many years ago I tried to explain the meaning of Christmas to a young man who had been raised in atheistic Communist China. He had never been exposed to any religious concepts, and I could find no common ground from which to start. The more I tried to explain Christianity, the more irrational it sounded. For the first time I truly understood Saint Paul's admonition, "God hath chosen the foolish things of the world to confound the wise." My final and most successful approach was simply to answer his questions as honestly as I could, and leave it to the Holy Spirit to lead him to understanding. In writing these articles, I have tried to discern what questions people might normally ask about the various groups, and then answer them as honestly as I can.

Though this book is written from a Christian perspective, I have tried to be objective and nonjudgmental. Within each half of the book the sections are arranged, to the extent that this is possible, chronologically, according to the time at which each faith originated or developed into its current form. While many readers will wish to read the book in its entirety, some may use it simply as a reference, to "look up" one particular faith. For this reason it seemed important to make the discussion of each faith fairly self-contained, even if this resulted occasionally in repetition of information in the book as a whole.

As the series progressed, a friend wisecracked to me, "Sects, sects, sects! All you ever think of is sects!" I believe that was a subtle way of telling me, "Enough, already," and that it was time to bring the project to a conclusion.

I would like to thank the many people who, as followers of the various disciplines, agreed to read my articles and point out errors and omissions. To those who find more errors and omissions, my apologies — but enough, already.

PART ONE

THE MANY FACES OF BELIEF

HINDUISM

The term "Hinduism" properly refers to the culture of the many ethnic and tribal groups living in the region south of the Indus River, and in the mountains northeast of India. Since similar beliefs and traditions generally pervade all of these groups, the syncretism of their religions is commonly referred to as Hinduism. It is most strongly represented in India and Nepal, although it is practiced worldwide, embracing one sixth of the world population. Hinduism not only values belief and intellectual understanding, but places at least an equal value on human relationships and the personal experience of divine truths. It can thus be considered both a religion and a philosophy. The origins of Hinduism are obscured in the mists of history, although there is evidence that it has roots in the teachings of the sage Vaasa in about 3000 BCE.[1] Hinduism as it is known today arose about 1500 BCE from a synthesis of the sacrificial cults of the Aryan invaders of India and the religion of the highly civilized Harappa culture of the Indus Valley. It has also been influenced in later times by Zoroastrianism, Judaism, Christianity, Islam, and several Asian religions including Chinese Taoism. Modern Hinduism owes much to Ramakrishna Paramahamsa (1834-86),

1. Because of the strength of Christian influence throughout the centuries, most of the world calculates dates in the eras before and after Christ. Traditionally this has been indicated as B.C. ("Before Christ") and A.D. (*Anno Domini*, "in the year of the Lord"). It is unreasonable, however, to expect a non-Christian to use *Anno Domini*. Out of respect for non-Christians most writers today use the terms CE (either "Christian era" or "common era") and BCE ("before the common era.")

who regenerated Hindu worship when it was in a serious decline after the British conquest of India.

The most apparent characteristics of Hinduism are a caste system and the acceptance of the Vedas (pronounced "VAY-duhs") as sacred scriptures. The modern Indian democratic government has abolished the caste system as a legal social structure, but it is still an integral part of Hindu spiritual thought. The Vedas contain the oldest known religious writings in any Indo-European language and are still accepted today by Hindus as the authoritative statement of the basic truths of Hinduism. Its root is the literature of the Aryans, fierce tribes from southern Russia who invaded the Indus Valley and settled in the Punjab about 1500 BCE. The Vedas, as a synthesis of the Aryan writings and the ideas and beliefs of the indigenous peoples of India, were compiled over a period of five centuries from about 1000-500 BCE. The "Vedic Sacrifice" involves the supplication of any of thirty-three gods through mantras (repetitive hymns). Through the centuries this has become a very complicated rite, and it is now regarded as the fundamental agency of creation. The climax of the Vedas is the *Upanishads,* mystical works that state the relationship between the ultimate deity Brahman and the human soul. They define the Karma, the consequences (sufferings or blessings) that result from one's actions. These consequences are not immediate, but affect one's life in a future incarnation. A particularly grievous sinner, for example, will be reincarnated as a Pariah, an "Untouchable." One's Karma can be improved through proper prayer and sacrifice and through the spiritual, psychological, and physical discipline of any of the various forms of Yoga, "joining," through which one becomes more closely united with the primary deity, Brahman.

Hinduism has no formal theology that defines God, but in general it can be considered a "henotheistic" religion (acknowledging many gods, but worshiping only one). Most Hindus believe in Brahman, the one all-pervasive deity that energizes the whole universe. Some see this deity as a personal being, others as an impersonal spiritual force. Still others believe in one all-powerful deity who manifests himself as many different gods (avatars). In the strictest sense, however, Hinduism is not polytheistic (worshiping many gods). There is a trio of avatars consisting of Lord Brahma, the creator (not to be confused with Brahman, the all-pervading spirit); Vishnu, the preserver; and Shiva, the destroyer. (This is in no way parallel to the Christian concept of the Holy Trinity.) Each of these avatars also manifests himself as other avatars. Brahma is rarely worshiped. Shiva and Vishnu and his avatars (incarnations) Rama and Krishna are the most commonly worshiped gods, along with their wives, Durga (or Shakti,) Saraswati, and Laxmi respectively. The three wives are often worshiped collectively as the Divine Mother. All these deities are worshiped as one. This worship is referred to as *puja*, and is focused on an image made of gold, silver, bronze, or clay, depending upon one's financial position. Many Hindus also worship images of deities in the form of elephants, monkeys, and other animals. It should be made clear that they do not worship the animals, but the avatars who manifest themselves in the shapes of these animals. The basic philosophy is that since God pervades everything in creation, worship of anything is worship of him. This is a difficult concept for non-Hindus to grasp. Hindus, although they have many representations of gods and spirits, are not idol worshipers. To the Hindu these representations are simply the means of focusing one's prayers and meditations, much as Christians use symbols such as crucifixes and images of saints. Only those who are ignorant of the fundamental teachings of their faith slip into paganism by believing that the images themselves have power.

There are many divisions in Hinduism, but the three major sects are Saivism (worshipers of Shiva, mainly in the south of India), Vaishnavism (worshipers of Vishnu, in the north), and Shaktism (worshipers of Shakti, in the region around Calcutta). Reincarnation is a basic Hindu belief. (Reincarnation is theologically unacceptable to Christianity, although some who profess to be Christians believe in it.) Hindus believe that the soul experiences life in many successive physical bodies, and that through these "lives" it learns more and more of the lessons that lead to perfect understanding. When perfect spiritual purity is reached the soul attains *mukti* — it then is no longer subject to being pulled back into incarnation in a physical body. The ultimate goal is the achievement of Nirvana, the emancipation from ignorance and the extinction of all attachments. It is an ideal condition of rest, harmony, stability, and joy, in perfect communion with Brahman.

Hinduism has no commandments, and thus no formal religious law, although the principles set forth in the Vedas have the authority of law. The cow is sacred to all Hindus. The strictest observers will not take any life, even for food, and this position is supported in the sacred writings. Many, however, particularly in the north of India, do eat meat. About a quarter of all Hindus are strict vegetarians. Many non-Hindus are misled about vegetarianism. For example, it is not true that Hindus will not use the products of the cow — they rely heavily on dairy products. Hindus view the cow, the provider of milk and all its products, as the most giving of all creatures. To the Hindu, all living creatures are sacred, and the cow, because it is the gentle source of so much sustenance, is the symbol of life (much as Western cultures view the eagle as the symbol of power). Hindus also honor the cow's docility and apparent peacefulness.

Most Hindu women and many men wear the *pottu,* a dot on the forehead, symbolic of a third eye. This represents the spiritual insight that all Hindus seek to awaken through yoga. Traditionally women wear a black dot before marriage and a red one afterward, although that tradition is fading. Today many use a color to complement their sari, the silk wrapping used as a gown. There are many subtle variations of the dot to communicate one's sect and religious or social status.

According to tradition, mankind is directly descended from Brahma in four emanations, forming the castes. The *Brahmans* (priests and rulers) descended from his head; the *Shatryans* (warriors) from his breast; the *Vaissyas* (farmers and merchants) from his thighs; and the *Sudras* (mechanics and laborers) from his feet. Another caste, the *Pariahs* ("Untouchables"), were simply created by him, and are not his direct descendants. They are permitted to do only the most menial services, and until recently could be put to death for allowing their shadow to fall on anyone of a high caste. This social structure is rigid. A person, when he is reincarnated, is assigned to a caste by Shiva. Any mobility between castes is seen as an attempt to undermine the will of the god. It is a sin to give any help or comfort to a Pariah, because he is in that caste as a punishment for his acts in a previous life. The Brahmans are those who achieved the highest Karma in previous lives.

Hinduism did not have a significant direct influence on Christianity, but it strongly influenced two faiths that grew from it, Buddhism and Zoroastrianism. The latter strongly influenced early Christian thinking, particularly with regard to the dualism between good and evil that plays such a major role in the Christian concept of the apocalypse. (This dualistic idea is rare in Hindu thinking.) In modern times, variations of yoga have become very popular among Christians as means of teaching mental, physical, and spiritual discipline.

JUDAISM

Judaism is a worldwide faith, with the strongest concentration of Jews[1] being in Israel, central Europe, and the northeastern United States.[2] It is based on God's revelation to Abraham that he is the creator and ruler of the universe, and that he loves his creatures and demands righteousness of them. Judaism as both a religion and a culture can claim three primary founding fathers: Abraham (twenty-first century BCE), Moses (thirteenth century BCE), and Ezra (mid-fifth century BCE).

Avram ben-Terah was of a tribe in the Chaldees (Mesopotamia), possibly the Habiru tribe, sometime around 2000 BCE. He was the son of Terah, a pagan idol-maker. God called him to leave his city of Ur and go into the wilderness, where he would direct him further. Avram's name was changed from Av-ram (Abram, "exalted father") to Av-raham (Abraham, "father of multitudes") as a statement of God's promise in his covenant. As a sign of the covenant God commanded that he, all the males of his tribe, and all his male descendants be cir-

---

1. Some people are uncomfortable using the term "Jew," thinking of it as pejorative, and prefer the term "Hebrew" or "Jewish person." "Jew" is the correct term — these others are offensive to most Jews. Likewise, the term "Jewess" is offensive — "Jew" refers to male or female. "Hebrews" is most often used to refer to the descendants of Jacob in Egypt before their acceptance of the covenant, and later to the Jews who accepted Jesus as the Messiah.

2. Until the Holocaust (1933-45) the greatest concentration of Jews was in Europe.

cumcised. This was not an uncommon practice by many peoples at the time, but it represented to them only a rite of passage — a physical sign that a boy had endured pain and through it achieved the final requirement for manhood. In Judaism (as in Islam) it represents the achievement of spiritual maturity by being bound to the covenant.

Abraham practiced a primitive form of monotheism after leaving Ur — primitive in that he doubtless acknowledged many other gods, but believed that his God was the ruler of all of them, and that only he should be worshiped or heeded (this is properly called "henotheism" rather than monotheism). Abraham smashed his father's idols not so much as a statement that the gods they represented did not exist, but to express his belief that they were powerless.

Although a Hebrew, Moses, the second "founder" of Judaism, was raised as an Egyptian. He may have been exposed to a simple form of monotheism[3] by his Hebrew nurse, who he later learned was his mother. He learned about the covenant from his father-in-law Jethro after his exile in the desert. He led the Hebrew slaves to freedom, initiated the concept of the Law, and emphasized the importance of obedience.

Ezra was one of the primary shapers of Judaism as it existed in Jesus' time. After the fall of Babylon to the Persians in 539 BCE, the Jews were permitted to return to Jerusalem and were encouraged by the Persians to rebuild the temple and restore their religion. Ezra, along with Nehemiah, was one of the primary movers in this effort. His em-

---

3. Monotheism did not originate with Judaism. It appeared a number of times in ancient religions, but usually only fleetingly. One of the most significant early non-Judaic appearances was in Egyptian Atonism, the worship of the one god Aton, symbolized by the sun. It flourished briefly under the deformed Pharaoh Akhn-aton ("Aton Is God," fourteenth century BCE) who was probably assassinated by the powerful polytheistic Amonist priests. Upon his death his son-in-law, the nine-year-old Tutankh-aton ("I Worship Aton"), "King Tut," ascended the throne, and was forced by the priests to change his name to Tutankh-amon ("I Worship Amon"). Polytheism was restored, and the Atonists were slaughtered. Atonism went underground and survived, however, and was still secretly practiced in the time of Moses a century later. Moses may have been taught by Atonists during his youth in the palace. This would have made it easy for him to understand and accept the henotheistic religion of Abraham, taught to him by his father-in-law Jethro in the desert. (He had heard little of it in Egypt, as most of the Hebrews there had abandoned it and embraced Amonism.)

phasis was not on simple obedience, but on a personal relationship with God developed through temple worship. While a return to the Law was essential in his teachings, he sought the spirit of the Law rather than obedience to a book of rules.

Judaism as it has been practiced since the destruction of Jerusalem in 70 CE is strongly influenced by writings of the rabbinic scholars of the first two centuries CE. Modern Judaism can be referred to as Rabbinic Judaism, placing its emphasis on the synagogue and rabbis (basically, school and teachers) rather than on the temple and the hereditary priesthood. The relationship with God comes through personal experience, gained through study and deeds, guided (but not ruled) by rabbis (teachers).

The sacred book of Judaism is the Bible (Christians would refer to it as the Old Testament), which is a collection of law, history, prophecy, and songs of praise. The most essential part is the "Written Law" — the books of Genesis, Exodus, Leviticus, Numbers, and Deuteronomy. According to tradition, Moses was the author of these books, but today all but the most conservative Jews acknowledge that the Law (or "Torah") was in fact written by many, many authors over centuries of time. Judaism and Christianity are the only religions whose books contain a history of the people and their faith. Also considered a part of the Law is the "Oral Law," the Talmud, an authoritative collection of ancient rabbinic interpretations of the Written Law. Although written down, it is called the Oral Law because it is traditionally taught orally, and portions of it were transmitted orally for centuries. Also important for study are the *Midrashim*, books of commentaries on the Torah, dated 400-1200 CE. "The Watchword" of Judaism is the *Shema*, "Hear, O Israel, the Lord our God, the Lord is One." The Jewish faith is summed up in the *Yigdal*, a prayer incorporating thirteen principles of faith set forth by the great Spanish rabbi Maimonides (1135-1204 CE).

Early Judaism saw God as the chief and most powerful god, to whom all the other gods must defer. They referred to him as Elohim, a plural word, indicating a hint of polytheism, and he was considered very demanding and even vengeful. The early Jews also took a very anthropomorphic view of God, describing, for example, how he walked in the Garden of Eden in the cool of the evening. As it developed, Judaism began to teach that this God was the only God. He identified himself to Moses as *Eh'i'yeh*, "I Am," which evolved to *Yahweh*.

Because of a misunderstanding of a Jewish scribal tradition, early English translators corrupted this to *Jehovah*. As the faith matured, the Jews came to see their God as loving and merciful. This was unusual; most world religions in ancient times saw the gods as a threat, demanding obedience, not righteousness. The early anthropomorphism also quickly evolved into allegorical symbolism as the Jews became strictly monotheistic, believing in one God who is pure spirit. Judaism thus now teaches that there is only one God who is the creator of all things in the universe and who loves his worshipers and demands righteousness of them.

Judaic cosmology, the concept of creation, is simple: God created the universe, both the spirit and material world, out of chaos. Modern Judaism has little concern for the end of creation, although there is a thread throughout Judaic tradition of a final battle of good and evil ("Armageddon") at the ancient Jewish battleground of Megiddo. Likewise, a concept of Satan as a personal power of evil, an antithesis of God, is not a serious consideration in Judaism. These concepts are much more developed in Zoroastrianism, Islam, and Christianity. Unlike most other Eastern religions, Judaism teaches that God created humankind as an object of love rather than as a servant or toy. Early Judaism had a very primitive concept of an afterlife; life in this world and man's response to God was the primary concern. Later, a concept of a heaven developed. In Jesus' time there was considerable controversy over whether or not there was resurrection and/or some form of eternal life.

Jews see God as having full control of his creation but believe he has given humans freedom and responsibility for their own actions. Man's primary responsibility is obedience to God, but in being obedient to God he accepts a responsibility to his fellow men. The greatest joy is study and interpretation of Torah, because this is the way one comes to know God better and becomes closer to him. The greatest gifts that God gave mankind are life and intellect, and they are held in great reverence. The favorite traditional toast is *L'chayim*, "To Life," and learning is revered above all other human achievements. This is because it is believed that the greater the learning, the greater the ability to live by the Commandments. This concept has pervaded Jewish culture so deeply that it is basic even to nonreligious Jews.

Traditional Judaism looks forward to the coming of the *Moshiach*, "the anointed one," which has been Anglicized to "Messiah." (Many Jews do not like the use of the term "Messiah," because it is generally associated with the Christian claim that Jesus is the *Moshiach*.) Most scholars believe that the messianic concept was introduced in the eighth or ninth century BCE, although some argue that hints of it can be seen in the earliest Jewish writings. There is a great diversity of interpretations of the role of the *Moshiach*. Today, most see him as a human spiritual leader, anointed by God, who will so inspire mankind with his righteousness that people will be irresistibly drawn to God. An ancient view still accepted by many today is that he will be a great political leader descended from King David. He will win military and spiritual battles for Israel, rebuild the temple, and reign over the world from his throne in Jerusalem. The most conservative Orthodox Jews believe that when he comes he will establish the worldly state of Israel (Zion), and that any attempt to do so before that time (including the present Israel established in 1948) is blasphemy. The idea of the *Moshiach* being a savior who will redeem man's sins and win for him everlasting life is not a traditional Jewish interpretation, but is peculiarly Christian.

Until the Babylonian exile, Jews practiced animal sacrifice in the temple as the basis of their formal worship. Only a priest could offer sacrifice after the earliest days of Judaism, and priesthood depended on lineage more than on training. No one but a tiny group of ultra-conservative Jews today has any wish to return to temple sacrifice. In Babylonia, Jews were forbidden to sacrifice to God, but they were encouraged to educate. Thus started the institution of the synagogue (from the Greek for "calling together"), ostensibly a school but with a liberal dose of prayer and religious teaching. The Yiddish[4] word for "synagogue" is *shul* from the German *Schul*, "school." Worship in the home was very important even in early Judaism, and, unlike most ancient Eastern religions, the mother had an equal part with the father in the religious training of the children. Worship in the home, and education, play a much more important part in Judaism than in Christianity.

4. Yiddish (from the German *Jüdisch*, "Jewish") is a language spoken by about four million Jews throughout the world — few Jews speak Hebrew. It is based on German, Russian, Hebrew, and several eastern European languages. (Linguistically, it is classified in the Germanic group of languages.) Since the days of the exile, Hebrew has generally been used only in worship and study — the everyday tongue in Jesus' day was Aramaic.

Judaism, like Christianity (and all other major religions), is extremely fragmented.[5] The primary divisions are the Orthodox Jews, who adhere literally to the Law of Torah; the Conservative Jews, who adhere to Torah, but moderate their practice to fit better with modern life and thinking; and the Reform (not "Reformed") Jews, who are liberal in their modernizing of ancient thought and practice. Each of these divisions is broken into innumerable subgroups, although all honor Torah as the basis of their faith. The distinctions derive from their view of the source of Torah — whether it was "dictated" word for word by God, inspired by God's direct guidance of human thought, or derived from the needs and insights of humans as they grew in their relationship with God. (In much the same ways, conservative, moderate, and liberal Christians view the source of the Bible.)

The influence of Judaism on Christianity is obvious. Jesus did not renounce Judaism to "start a new religion." He was a faithful Jew whom Christians believe to be the fulfillment of the Law and the prophets — the Messiah — not the founder of a new faith. Judaism also had a strong influence on Islam. Muhammad based his teachings on those of Judaism and Christianity, and referred to Jews and Christians as "the people of the Book."

The Jews refer to themselves as the "Chosen People." This is not arrogance or elitism. It does not mean that Jews think God loves them more than anyone else, but that God has chosen them to prepare the way for the fallen world to return to him. This is an awesome responsibility, which faithful Jews seek to meet by establishing the closest possible relationship with God.

5. Like Christianity, Judaism became fragmented in its earliest days. The Edomites, descendants of Jacob's twin Esau, claimed to be Jews, but this claim was rejected by the Jews (King Herod was an Edomite). During the reign of King Ahab, the Jews of the Northern Kingdom developed practices corrupted by paganism and were also rejected — these were the Samaritans.

ZOROASTRIANISM

Zoroastrianism is one of the smallest of the major world religions in number of believers,[1] yet it is important because of its significant influence on many other religions, especially Christianity and Islam. It was founded by the Persian prophet Zarathushtra Spitama, who is better known by the Greek corruption of his name, Zoroaster. Little is known of his life, but his teachings are preserved in a collection of Gathas, metrical psalms written by him that form a part of the sacred scripture known as the Zend Avesta. He is believed to have lived sometime between 1700 and 1500 BCE in the easternmost Persian land of Airyana Vaejah.[2]

In order to appreciate Zoroastrian thinking it is necessary to understand the social conditions of Zarathushtra's time. The religion was one of the many pagan systems that typified Middle Eastern culture of the second millennium BCE. Society was divided into three classes: priests, warriors, and farmers (these classes later evolved into strict castes). There were particular gods called *daivas* ("heavenly ones") associated with each class. The *daivas* connected with the first class were

1. There are about 125,000 followers in India around the region of Bombay ("Parsees" or "Parsis"), and about 10,000 in Iran ("Gabrs" or "Guebre").

2. This is according to the latest findings by British researcher Mary Boyce and professor James Russell of Columbia University. Most current resources date him in the sixth to seventh centuries BCE, but this is based on the fact that Zoroastrianism first became known to the rest of the world during the Achaemenid Dynasty in Persia (the time of Cyrus the Great).

called *ahuras* ("lords").[3] The *ahuras* were inimical to the rest of the *daivas*.[4] Zarathushtra introduced monotheism to his region by rejecting the cults of all these gods but one, whom he called Ahura Mazda ("Wise Lord" or "Ormuzd"). Ahura Mazda's symbols are fire, light, and the sun. Zarathushtra also introduced the concept of ethical dualism, a conflict between the power of good and the power of evil. He identified these as opposite mental states of Ormuzd, calling them *Spenta Mainyu* ("Righteous Spirit") and *Angra Mainyu* ("Destructive Spirit").[5] Somewhat later tradition crystallized the latter into the concept of the arch-nemesis of Ahura Mazda — Ahriman, the quintessence of all that is evil, whose symbols are cold, darkness, and fear.

This ethical dualism, the ongoing conflict between good and evil, is basic to Zoroastrian thought through most of the history of the faith. It had a major influence on Christianity — the conflict can be seen in the Book of Revelation, for example — and on Islam.

Zoroastrianism's dualism of good and evil is symbolized in a legend, according to which the history of the universe was divided into four 3000-year cycles. After the first 3000 years Ahriman crossed the void and attacked Ormuzd. Ormuzd, recognizing that the conflict could last for eternity, made a pact with Ahriman that there would be a limit on their battle. He then uttered the *Ahuna Vairya*, the most sacred of all prayers, and the horrified Ahriman fell back to the darkness, where he lay defeated for another 3000 years. During this time Ormuzd created the world and mankind. Meanwhile Ahriman created six demons and all the woes he would introduce into Ormuzd's creation. At the end of this period Ahriman, instigated by the Primeval Woman, burst through the sky and introduced his corruption into Ormuzd's creation, thus forcing humans to choose between good and evil. The corrupt era lasted for 3000 years, at the end of which Zarathushtra was born and ushered in the final 3000-year era.

At the end of each thousand years of this last era, a posthumous son of Zarathushtra will be born and will be a savior who will bring

---

3. One of the very important *ahuras* was Mithra, the god of light and wisdom, whose cult later became very strong in Rome. In the second century CE in Rome there were more Mithraists than Christians.

4. The term *daiva* comes from the same ancient Indo-European root as "devil."

5. George Lukas in *Star Wars* drew on this type of dualism in his concept of the Force and the Dark Side of the Force, two aspects of the same power.

mankind closer to righteousness. The third and last of these sons (or *saoshyants,* "saviors") will bring about the final conflict in which Ahriman will be eternally defeated and all good creation will be merged into infinite time with Ormuzd. Zoroastrians anticipate his coming much as Jews await the coming of the Messiah, except that in Zoroastrianism the conditions of his advent are more clearly defined. At the end of the universe there will be a great conflagration that will destroy the world. All good souls will achieve a state of perfect harmony with (or absorption into) Ormuzd, awaiting a new creation (consider the Hindu belief in nirvana). Until the final conflict between good and evil, humans at death pass over the Bridge of the Requiter, where they are judged. The righteous wait there to be led into heaven, and the evil are cast off the bridge into the pit of darkness with Ahriman. There are obvious parallels between this legend and the Judeo-Christian legend of the rebellion of Lucifer, his introduction of evil into the world in the Garden of Eden, and his ultimate defeat at Armageddon.

After the death of Zarathushtra his teachings began to spread south into what is now Afghanistan and then from there westward into the land of the Medes and Persians. During this spread the religion suffered some noticeable contamination from local pagan beliefs that were absorbed and converted to Zoroastrian symbolism; this is similar to the injection of many originally pagan practices into Christianity, notably many of our Christmas customs. Zoroastrianism first flourished under the Achaemenid Dynasty (539-330 BCE), and reached the height of its popularity during the reign of Cyrus the Great, the Persian emperor who conquered Babylon and freed the Jews. Cyrus supported the Jews' return to Judea and the restoration of the temple in Jerusalem. During this period the Jews were in close contact with the Persians, and there was doubtless a significant influence of Zoroastrianism on Judaism. While the dualism of good versus evil powers was never a strong belief in Judaism, it first appeared during the post-exilic era, and it was at this time that the legends of the fall of Lucifer first crystallized in Jewish tradition.[6]

---

6. As is evident in the book of Job, Satan in early Judaic thought was seen as something of an agent of God, tempting the righteous in order to test their faith. It was not until the later post-exilic era that the idea of Satan as the evil antithesis of God appeared.

After Alexander's conquest of Persia the empire became strongly Hellenized, and the pagan religions of the Mediterranean spread throughout the Middle East. Zoroastrianism fell into decline. It did not see a serious revival until the defeat of the Parthians and the establishment of a new Persian Empire in 224 CE. With the ascent to the throne of the distinctly Persian Sasanian Dynasty, Zoroastrianism was declared the official religion of the empire. The dualistic "Mazdean" doctrine was declared official, replacing the early pure monotheism of Zarathushtra's Gathas. Other religions in the region, primarily Christianity and Buddhism, were suppressed. Zoroastrianism is generally very tolerant of other religions, but at this time Armenian Christians were aggressively trying to convert Zoroastrians and were burning their temples. They were encouraged by the Romans who, up to that time, had been kept out of Asia by the Persians, and were glad to help crush anything Persian. Zoroastrianism, now the official religion, suppressed these others in order to defend itself from their hostility.

With the rise of Islam in the seventh century CE, Zoroastrianism was at first tolerated, but persecution developed and intensified as Islam strengthened. By the end of the tenth century, persecution and forced conversion to Islam led many of the remaining Zoroastrians to flee to India, most of them settling in the area around Bombay. By the nineteenth century these people, known as Parsees, were leading citizens, noted not only for their wealth and education but also for their generosity and piety. In the late nineteenth century they established strong communication with the Zoroastrians who remained in Persia (now Iran), who were known as Gabrs or Guebre (from an Old Arabic term for "infidel"). The Gabrs were tolerated and even respected during the reign of the Shahs, but with the rise of fundamentalist Islam under the present regime they are scorned and oppressed.

The most significant visible characteristic of Zoroastrian worship is the tending of a fire sweetened with sandalwood in every home and in the temple. The sacred fire is symbolic of the light and eternal presence of Ahura Mazda and is revered as the great purifier, bearing the nature of the sun itself.

Zoroastrian sacred writings fall into two categories: the Avesta, the original work written in the early Persian language of Avestan (a derivative of Sanskrit) and containing the Gathas; and a collection of much later texts written in Pahlavi, a dialect of Middle Persian that is an early form of the modern Iranian language. The most recent portion of the Avesta, the Vendidad, was composed after Alexander's conquest of Persia in 330 BCE. It is mainly a codex of ritual and law, and is in many ways similar to the Old Testament book of Leviticus. The influence of Zoroastrianism on Judaism and Christianity is apparent in some of the legends mentioned above, but there is one more important connection between Zoroastrianism and Christianity. No one is sure of the identity of the "wise men from the east" who followed the star to visit Jesus at his birth; that they were kings and that there were three of them is a late medieval tradition with no scriptural authority. Matthew calls them *magoi* (Latinized to *magi*, a term generally only applied to members of the Zoroastrian priestly caste from Persia. Magi were powerful and scholarly men who studied astrology very seriously — a new star in the sky would obviously be of great importance to them. Christians celebrate their visit to the Christ child on Epiphany, January 6, "The Feast of the Manifestation of Christ to the Gentiles." We interpret it as the first sign that Jesus came for all mankind, and not just for the Jews.

Zoroastrianism is a faith that is generally held in respect by Christians, not only because of the tie with Epiphany and the similarity of much of the legendry, but also because it is a religion whose adherents place great value on truth, piety, and a life of peace.

TAOISM AND CONFUCIANISM

There are three major spiritual philosophies practiced in China today — Taoism, Confucianism, and Buddhism. The first two are atheistic in their pure form. Buddhism, which originated in India rather than in China, is essentially agnostic. (We will deal with Buddhism separately in the next chapter.) It is reasonable to say that for millennia before the atheistic Communist revolution of 1949, China was a nation without real religion. Its culture had developed around these philosophies, liberally flavored with superstition and a touch of paganism. An important concept in much of Asian thinking is the *Yang-yin*. Yang, "sun," is the male principle. It is bright, active, dominant, and good. Yin, "moon," the female element, is dark, damp, cold, passive, and evil. All things (including people) have both, and their degree of good or evil is a function of their balance of yang and yin. This balance can vary. When a tree with a strong yang dies, it loses much of its yang force and becomes rotten, moist, and more yin. If a good human becomes corrupt and evil, he has allowed the yin force in him to become dominant.[1]

---

1. This is reminiscent of the dualism of good and evil that is found in Zoroastrianism and Christianity. Yang and yin can also be thought of as much like the "Force" and "Dark Side" in *Star Wars* — paired yet opposite. The main difference is that the "Force" is an active power to be called upon, while yang-yin is completely passive and must be approached.

Taoism

Taoism (pronounced "dow-ism," rhyming with "now") is not a religion in the strict sense, but rather a religious philosophy. It is based on the concept of the *Tao*, the "Way" or "Path," the simple but mysterious way of the universe.[2] As it is practiced in China today, its original teachings have become quite corrupted with paganism, polytheism, and magic. The founder of Taoism is believed to be Lao-tse (pronounced "Low-dzuh," "Low" rhyming with "now" and "dzuh" with "the"), whose name means "Ancient One" or "Old Sage." He may be more a legend than a real historical character, although it is possible that he was a royal librarian named Li Erh, born about 604 BCE. In his old age Lao-tse became disgusted with the corruption of society and traveled west to find solitude. Before he disappeared into the unknown western regions of Asia a gatekeeper asked him to write down his philosophy. This book, known as the *Tao-te-ching* ("Way of Classic Virtue"), consists of eighty-one short poems on the meaning of the Tao. Like John's Gospel, its language appears simple upon a first reading, but is exquisitely subtle and allows several levels of interpretation and exegesis. It is doubtful that Lao-tze intended deep and subtle meaning to his poems. Some of the modern interpretations of the *Tao-te-ching* would probably amaze him — as T. S. Eliot quipped after hearing a group of students analyze one of his own poems, "I had no idea I was so profound!"

The essence of Taoism is simplicity. The Tao, the Way of the Universe, cannot be defined, but must be discerned. It is discovered by observing the actions of things that are allowed to proceed in their own natural way, with no human interference — the flight of a bird, the flow of a stream, the growth of a flower. The damming of a river, the building of a road or house, even the plowing of a field interfere with the Tao and lead to evil and disharmony. The ideal is a negative approach, the *wu-wei*, the "not doing." The modern expression would be to "go with the flow." A drunken man can fall down without getting hurt because he does not tense up and resist the natural course of the fall. He simply follows the Tao.

Taoism places great value on life. It does not focus on life after

---

2. The word *Tao*, "way," has the same root as the word *do* that ends the names of many martial arts: *ju-do*, "soft way," and *tai-kwon-do*, "way of the trampling fist."

death, but emphasizes the health and longevity that can be acquired by living a life of simplicity and inner peace. This requires minimal government, peaceful coexistence between states, and total nonaggression and nonviolence. Weapons and any tools of violence are to be detested. Only those who follow the Tao and give up any desire to control can become great leaders. Lao-tze wrote, "The Sage manages affairs without action; preaches the doctrine without words. . . . He acts, but does not appropriate; accomplishes, but claims no credit. It is because he lays claim to no credit that the credit cannot be taken away from him" (*Tao-te-Ching,* chapter 2). Taoism is strictly monistic in that it rejects the separateness of the forces of yang and yin. It does accept them, however, as aspects of the activity of the one universal Tao. The ultimate goal is the return to the Tao by transforming the conflict of yang-yin into a harmonious mode. This is accomplished by withdrawing from any activity that interferes with the normal flow of nature. "The Tao never does, yet through it everything is done" (*Tao-te-Ching,* chapter 37). The Tao, "the Way," can be summarized in the writing of Lao-tze in the *Tao-te-ching:* "Act without doing, work without effort. . . . Confront the difficult while it is still easy; accomplish the great task by a series of small acts. The master never reaches for the great, and thus achieves greatness. . . . Prevent trouble before it arises. Put things in order before they exist. The giant pine tree grows from a tiny sprout. The journey of a thousand miles starts with the first step" (chapters 63, 64).

Confucianism

Confucianism, like Taoism, is not a religion but a philosophy. It has been the major system of thought in China for millennia and is concerned with the principles of good conduct, practical wisdom, and proper social relationships. It is based on the teachings of the philosopher K'ung Fu-tze, better known to us as Confucius[3] (551-479 BCE), one of the most important characters in Chinese history and a contemporary of Lao-tze. His teachings, put into writing by his disciples, fill about twelve volumes (as opposed to the five thousand words of the

---

3. His true name was K'ung Ch'iu. His teachings earned him the title K'ung Fu-tze, "K'ung the Great Sage." In the Western world this epithet has been Latinized to Confucius.

Tai-te-ching), but the most important is the *Lun Yü,* "The Analects." A book that is often incorrectly attributed to Confucius is the *I Ching (The Book of Changes)*. This became very popular among the "flower children" of the 1960s and '70s. It is an eleventh-century BCE book of divination, to which Confucius added a commentary.

There are no deities in Confucianism, nor is there any priesthood or organization. The few Confucian "temples" are nothing more than public meeting places used for ceremonies and celebrations. The central construct of Confucianism is *jen,* translated as "love," "goodness," or "humanity." *Jen* is the supreme virtue, representing the finest of human qualities. It is manifested in *chung,* faithfulness to oneself and others, and *shu,* altruism, expressed in the Confucian teaching, "Do not do to others what you do not want done to yourself." Confucius also set guidelines for those in power, teaching that "they must be benevolent and honorable, and their subjects respectful and obedient." He also taught that in education there must be no class distinction (an amazing teaching considering the feudal society in which he lived).

There are two major areas of Confucian thought. The first, "The Great Learning," is concerned with social and political structure. The second, "The Doctrine of the Mean," is a teaching that emphasizes the full realization of the self through the harmony of the emotions, and the development of all actions in the light of their harmonious relationships. Sincerity and honesty are basic to all humans. Only those who are truly sincere can develop fully their own natures, the natures of others, and the nature of things. Only through sincerity can we participate in the great harmony of heaven and earth. The goal is the attainment of *chün-tze,* the state of the perfect individual functioning in a flawlessly ordered society. After the death of Confucius two schools of thought developed, one taught by Meng-tze (Mencius, 371?-289? BCE) and the other by Hsün-tze (300?-235? BCE). Mencius continued Confucius's teaching that human nature is innately good, but corruptible. Hsün-tze taught the opposite, that mankind is basically evil but can be reformed with moral education.

Neither Taoism nor Confucianism is honored by the present Communist state in China. At first Mao Tse-tung tried to suppress them, but he soon realized that they were too deeply ingrained in Chinese thinking and society to do so. They are now officially tolerated but discouraged, yet it is patently evident that Confucian teaching is very much a part of the thinking of many of the current Chinese leaders.

BUDDHISM

Buddhism, although it originated in India, is practiced by vast populations throughout the Asian continent and enjoys a strong following in every country on earth. In Myanmar (Burma) and Thailand it is the religion of 90 percent of the population; about 60 percent of Japanese and 17 percent of Chinese[1] are Buddhists, and it is by far the prominent belief of most of southeast Asia. While there are many gods loosely associated with Buddhism (Buddha himself is not seen as a god), it is essentially an agnostic philosophy rather than a true religion. Very little attention is paid to any deity — the gods are seen as having created the universe and as exerting some influence in it, but only in a very passive way. Far more important than any theology is the philosophical and spiritual teaching of Buddha.

The man called Buddha was Siddhartha Gautama (563?-483? BCE), a prince of a small Hindu kingdom on the India-Nepal border. His mother died soon after his birth. His father, fearing the prophecies that Siddhartha would become a great sage and renounce the throne, kept him a virtual prisoner in the palace, surrounding him with luxury. The young prince was constantly watched to insure that he would never experience pain, poverty, suffering, old age, or death. When he was twenty-nine years old he discovered a secret gate in the palace wall.

---

1. This is an extraordinarily high percentage when one considers not only the enforced atheism of the Communist regime, but also the fact that China has been an essentially atheistic culture for thousands of years.

His curiosity led him to go through it, and he found himself in the city. There he saw grief, poverty, sickness, and death — evils he had never before encountered. On a second excursion into the city he met a band of wandering ascetics and was fascinated by their quest for enlightenment. Leaving behind his wife and baby, he slipped out of the palace and joined the ascetics, determined to discover a way for mankind to escape suffering. For six years, clothed only in rags, he fasted almost to the point of starvation. He devoted himself wholly to meditation, never bathing, and taking only enough time from his meditation to beg in order to keep himself barely alive.

After six years Siddhartha realized that no one could transcend suffering by suffering,[2] and he espoused what he called the Middle Path — a life of self-discipline and introspection, but not of self-flagellation. He likened life to a string on a musical instrument — it will not play if it is too tight or too loose, but at the proper tension it will make beautiful music that will enlighten others. He bathed and resumed eating and soon was restored to good health. He sat under a fig tree[3] and vowed not to stand upright until he had achieved an understanding of spirituality. Although raised a Hindu, he rejected Vedic Hinduism. Nevertheless, he retained many of the Hindu concepts, particularly the ideas of reincarnation, nonviolence, and compassion. During his meditations he attained understanding of all his previous lives, and he could perceive the Karma (see below) of those around him. He finally reached a spiritual state that released him from *samsara*, the eternal cycle of death and reincarnation — he had attained *bodhi*, "enlightenment," and was thereafter known as Buddha, "the Enlightened One."

Buddha taught the Four Noble Truths:

1. All existence is pain.
2. All pain is caused by human cravings.
3. The relinquishing of and detachment from craving will cease pain.
4. There is an eightfold path that leads to the cessation of pain: right view, right thought, right speech, right action, right livelihood, right effort, right mindfulness, and right concentration.

2. This belief is somewhat contradicted by the teaching of many Tantric (*Vajrayana*) Buddhists, who are described later in this section.

3. It was a peepul tree (*ficus religiosa*), a fig species found in India. It is sacred to Buddhists, who call it a *bodhi* ("enlightenment") tree.

Man is in a constant state of transition, in which every thought, word, and deed has its own consequence called Karma. He is constantly reincarnated until he reaches a stage of perfection where his actions have only good Karma. At this point he is released from *samsara* and enters nirvana, a state of pure objective wisdom and compassion. In nirvana he comes into total unity with *Dharma*, the essential nature of the universe.

There are five major Buddhist schools of thought. These are differing traditions rather than sects, as each focuses on different aspects of Buddha's teaching rather than being the result of disagreement or heresy:

(1) *Theravada*, "The Way of the Elders": This school claims to practice the original teachings of Buddha. Its primary scriptures date back to the second century BCE and are interpreted absolutely literally. The followers of Theravada embrace the Hindu caste system, believing that one's caste is a reflection of his Karma in his previous life. Only those who have reached the Brahmin caste can attain enlightenment, so there is no need to waste time teaching the other castes anything more than what is needed to learn to achieve good Karma. Enlightenment can only be attained by those who dedicate themselves wholly to seeking it, such as monks. Those who have achieved it have no obligation to help others to that end.

(2) *Mahayana*, "The Greater Vehicle": This school claims to represent the final teachings of Buddha, carried to the world by his most dedicated disciples, who had been sworn to secrecy until his teachings and their understanding of them were complete. It teaches reincarnation as a hierarchy of lives with the achievement of Buddhahood (enlightenment) as the last stage. Those who are rising toward Buddhahood are known as *Bodhisattva*. They dedicate themselves to aiding any aspirant to enlightenment, regardless of caste. The highest form of compassion is exhibited by those Bodhisattva who delay their own enlightenment in order to be available to help others toward that goal.

(3) *Zen (Ch'en):* Zen is a late Sino-Japanese school of Mahayana Buddhism. It focuses on meditation as the route to enlightenment and is thus an essentially monastic discipline. Its practitioners believe that enlightenment can best be attained by understanding oneself, and they place great importance on introspection and self-control. The Western oversimplification of this is described as "contemplating one's navel."

Some Zen practitioners arrange to have themselves occasionally struck with a *keisaku*, a broad wooden paddle that is painful and makes a loud slapping noise when it strikes the flesh. The purpose is not to experience pain, but to learn not to let pain or noise interrupt one's meditations. While the practice of Zen requires great self-discipline, it is a spiritual and mental discipline, not a physical one. Zen became popular in America during the 1960s, but most American Zen bears little resemblance to Asiatic Buddhism, being based more on esoteric philosophical ideas and Hindu Yoga than on the attainment of enlightenment. There is, however, a growing popularity of Zen as it is practiced in Asia among those of non-Asian heritage in America. There are even many Zen monasteries here.

(4) *Vajrayana*, "The Diamond Vehicle," also known as Tantric Buddhism: This form of Buddhism is based on the Tantras, a series of comparatively recent texts believed to have originated in India. They deal mainly in mysticism and magic. Tantric Buddhists believe that all action is a form of meditation, and that we can learn and grow even from actions that are objectively thought of as unproductive or even evil.[4] They believe that it is possible to obtain enlightenment in a single lifetime by identifying one's personal thoughts and actions with those of the Buddha.

(5) *Amitabha* or *Amidism*, "Pure Land" Buddhism: This is also a later school, and like the Mahayana is compassionate, seeking to help others achieve enlightenment. The goal is to come to a "pure land," a state of rebirth in which one is not encumbered with the bad Karma of previous lives and can thus devote oneself completely to seeking enlightenment. This tradition makes great use of chants, mantras, and repetitive recitations in order to focus on enlightening thoughts and meditations.

From the time of Buddha himself his most dedicated followers organized themselves into monastic groups called *sanghas*, identifying themselves by shaven heads and unsewn yellow robes (in the Asian tradition yellow is the color of sorrow or mourning, as black is in the

---

4. Some Tantrics have corrupted this concept and seek enlightenment by indulging in sex, alcohol, and licentiousness, and occasionally by dabbling in magic. They argue that as a thorn can be used to remove another thorn, so a wise man can use licentiousness to purify his life (which is reminiscent of the sacred prostitution in the temples in the ancient Middle East).

Western tradition). In the early days they were wanderers, settling into one place only during the rainy season if at all. In later years they established temples and monasteries. These groups are democratic and independent of one another, having no central rule or structure other than the teachings of Buddha. In some, particularly in Japan, the monks are allowed to marry and raise families. Begging is discouraged — the monks are expected to work in the fields or at a trade in order to support themselves and their community. In Tibet the monasteries are all centrally organized under the Dalai Lama, the "All-encompassing Monk," who is believed to be a spiritual descendent of Buddha.

Starting many centuries ago some of these communities began practicing physical agility and exercise as a means of mental and physical self-discipline. Some of these systems developed into modern martial arts such as jiu-jitsu and k'ung-fu. To be consistent with their Buddhist origins these arts must be used only for self-discipline and self-defense, and never aggressively. Lay worship is individual, rarely corporate. Worship as we think of it is not common or required. Spiritual union with higher powers is expressed in the self-discipline and meditation that leads to enlightenment. While belief in God or gods is not inconsistent with Buddhism, it is not an important aspect of it. A common expression of faith is the "Three Refuges": "I take refuge in the Buddha. I take refuge in the Dharma. I take refuge in the Sangha." Buddhism is a constantly growing and developing system. Throughout its history it has adapted itself to the culture of the local region, resulting in distinctly Indian, Chinese, Tibetan, Korean, and other traditions. It is not unlikely that as awareness of and interest in Buddhism grows in America there will eventually develop a distinctly American form of Buddhism. Buddhism has had little influence on other religions, but it has played an important part in the development of most Asian cultures. It is a peaceful and meditative religion, espousing the highest concepts of self-discipline and compassionate human relations.

however, both Khadija and Abu Talib died, and Muhammad lost the last of his support. Many of his followers fled to the nearby city of Yathrib, which welcomed them. Finally on July 16, 622, a plot against his life forced him to leave Mecca and flee with the last of his disciples to Yathrib. This flight is called the hegira or hijra and is considered to be the beginning of Islam as a religion. All Muslim dates are calculated from this date and are designated A.H., "the year of hijra." The name of Yathrib was changed to *Medina*, "City," implying "the city of the prophet." There Muhammad became the spiritual and political leader of the city. In 623 he married nine-year-old Aisha,[4] the daughter of his powerful advisor Abu Bakr, in order to secure more strength and power in the city. He married several other women in future years, but Aisha, although childless, remained his favorite wife until his death.

As the city expanded there arose a need for food and other supplies. Muhammad permitted the raiding of any caravans not owned by Muslims, and allowed most of the loot to be kept by the raiders.[5] Needless to say, converts flooded into Medina in order to participate in this rapine. Eventually Muhammad became such a menace in the region that Mecca raised a large army to destroy the Muslims. Somehow, although outnumbered, the Muslim army routed the Meccans and took this as a sign that Allah blessed their activities. This encouraged the doctrine of jihad, holy war, which permitted the Muslims to conquer infidels by military might and force their conversion to Islam. In the centuries that followed Muslim armies swept west across southern Europe and northern Africa, converting whole populations at sword-point. Up to that time the Jews and Christians had been tolerant and even supportive of Muhammad and his followers, but with the beginning of jihad they turned against them. Muhammad was now strong enough that he no longer needed their support, however, and simply dismissed them as more enemies. His army attacked and took Mecca. He established a shrine there, the *Ka'ba*, and dedicated it as a worldwide center

---

4. Marriages to young children for the purpose of uniting important families were not rare in those days in Arabic countries. Sexual relations, however, were generally deferred until the child had reached maturity.

5. It must be said in his defense that this was a part of the Arabic culture of the time. Life in that arid corner of the world was so difficult that individuals became wholly focused on their own families and tribes. Conquest of rival tribes was a sign of virility and often a means of survival, and was highly honored in the culture.

for religious pilgrimage or *hajj*. Every Muslim in the world is required, if at all possible, to make a *hajj* to Mecca at least once in his life.

In 632 Muhammad died of old war wounds. Muslim legend has it that his spirit rode his horse to Jerusalem and onto the holy rock on Mount Moriah (where the temple had stood), where he and his horse rode straight into heaven. The leadership of Islam was given to his father-in-law Abu Bakr (573-634), the first *h'alifah* (caliph, "successor") of the Muslim Empire. He died two years later, and Umar I was selected as caliph. Under the leadership of the three caliphs who succeeded Muhammad — Abu Bakr, Umar, and Uthman ibn Affan — the empire continued its astonishingly rapid expansion throughout the Arab world, by both voluntary conversion and military conquest. In 656 Muhammad's son-in-law Ali ibn Abi Talib became caliph. He had been strongly opposed by Aisha, who had organized an armed revolt against him. In 661 Ali was assassinated, precipitating a major schism in Islam between the Shi'ites, followers of Ali, and the Sunnites, fundamentalist adherents of orthodox Islam as presented in the Qur'an. That division survives to this day. At the time the schism was purely political, but in the ensuing years a distinct Shi'ite theology evolved.

Islamic Teachings

The Arabs refer to themselves as Ishmaelites, claiming descent from Ishmael, the son of Abraham and the Egyptian slave Hagar. Muslims believe that Allah revealed himself partially many times before the time of Muhammad, and that the two major partial revelations were in the Old and New Testaments. His revelation was not complete, however, until the Qur'an. The Qur'an was dictated literally to Muhammad by Gabriel and is an exact copy of the original, which is in heaven.[6] No translation, therefore, is adequate for the promulgation of doctrine, which must be taken directly from the Arabic. The Qur'an consists of 114 suras (chapters), arranged in descending order by

---

6. This is similar to the Mormon belief that the golden tablets of the Book of Mormon were given to Joseph Smith by the Angel Moroni. Smith wrote down the translation with divine help, and then the golden plates were assumed back into heaven.

length. They are in poetic form, containing many obscure allusions. Because of this it is possible to glean conflicting theological interpretations from almost any major passage. For example, the Qur'an forbids the taking of hostages, yet the Shi'ite Ayatollah Khomeini interpreted this to mean only Shi'ite hostages. Thus his conscience was clear in taking Sunnite and non-Muslim hostages. Qur'anic theology is rigidly monotheistic. Allah is unique, omnipotent, and merciful. He demands that all men obey him (in other words, become Muslim). There are five basic articles of faith: (1) belief in one God; (2) belief in angels as his emissaries; (3) literal belief in the teachings of the Qur'an; (4) trust in the prophets, particularly the chief prophet Muhammad; and (5) belief in the Day of Judgment. The faith is summed up in the *Shahada*, "There is no God but Allah, and Muhammad is his prophet." All Muslims are required to practice the "Five Pillars of Islam": (1) to recite the full profession of faith at least once in one's lifetime; (2) to pray the five daily public collective prayers; (3) to pay the *zakat*, the "purification tax" for the support of the poor; (4) to fast from sunrise to sunset every day during the month of Ramadan; and (5) if at all physically and financially possible, to perform the *hajj* (pilgrimage to Mecca) at least once.

The basis of Islamic practice is the *Shari'ah*, the Law. It embodies the total doctrine, discipline, and practice of Islam. As Orthodox Jews adhere to Torah, fundamentalist Muslims believe that *Shari'ah* governs every possible human thought and action. *Shari'ah* was formulated by Muslim religious leaders during the eighth and ninth centuries CE, and preceded the formulation of any systematic Muslim theology. It requires strict dietary discipline — Muslims are, for example, allowed no pork, alcohol, or tobacco. It establishes males as clearly superior to females, who are in most Islamic societies treated like slaves or possessions. Men are allowed great sexual freedom, but the standards of modesty and morality for women are rigid and strictly enforced.

Islamic Groups

Islam is as severely fragmented as any other major world religion. The primary branches today are the Shi'ites (those who believed that Muhammad's son-in-law Ali should have been the fourth caliph), the Sunnis or Sunnites (orthodox fundamentalists), and the Sufis, an ascetic warrior group of orthodox Muslims who were primarily respon-sible for the conquest and conversion of India, central Asia, Turkey, and central Africa.

The "Nation of Islam"

In 1913 Wali Farad Muhammad (born Wallace Fard) founded the "Lost-Found Nation of Islam" (known as the "Black Muslims"), claim-ing that Christianity was a "white man's religion" and that most of the slaves brought to this country had been taken from Muslim countries in Africa (which is true only to a limited extent). In 1934 the movement was taken over by Elijah Muhammad (born Elijah Poole). It was not an important force until 1952, when Malcolm X (born Malcolm Little) be-came Elijah Muhammad's main spokesman. During the 1960s Civil Rights era vast numbers of blacks joined the movement. Malcolm be-came disillusioned with what he claimed was unconscionable corrup-tion and politics, and in 1965 left the movement to become an ortho-dox Muslim. He began to speak well of Martin Luther King's principle of nonviolence, with which he had previously disagreed, and soon thereafter he was assassinated. Leadership was taken over by Louis Farrakhan (born Louis Wolcott), who assumed full control after the death of Elijah Muhammad. He has made many inflammatory racist, anti-Semitic, and anti-American statements that are highly offensive to many Muslims and most non-Muslims. Most branches of Islam do not consider the Nation of Islam to be a true Muslim movement, but a po-litical one under the guise of Islam. Many adherents of the Nation of Islam, however, are devout believers in the teachings of Islam.

MORMONISM

The Church of Jesus Christ of Latter-day Saints

Mormonism, the Church of Jesus Christ of Latter-day Saints (often referred to as LDS), is a major world religion with over eight million members, about half of whom live in the United States. It is not an orthodox Christian denomination, but rather a separate religion with roots in Christianity.[1] Its founding was based on the precept that Christianity was corrupt and thus invalidated, and that God restored it with a new revelation. Mormons call themselves restorationist Christians, but orthodox Christians, while admiring many aspects of Mormon social practice, consider Mormonism a major heresy or a cult. There are several serious doctrinal reasons for this that will be explained below, not the least of which is that Mormonism is polytheistic. Mormons support religious toleration and see value in all religions, but they maintain that theirs is "the only true and living church on earth," with exclusive claim to truth and revelation. They believe that ever since Mormonism was revealed in 1830, God has ceased speaking to mankind in matters of faith except through the Mormon church, and there only through its top leadership, the prophet (president) and the "first presidency." Mormons believe that God guides individuals in matters of personal deci-

---

1. The tie of Mormonism to Christianity is somewhat similar to the tie of Christianity to Judaism. Christianity grew out of Judaism, and the two faiths share some scriptures, but their theologies of redemption and salvation are quite different. Christianity sees itself as the fulfillment of Judaism, however, while Mormonism sees itself as a replacement of traditional Christianity. It is as unreasonable to call a Mormon a Christian as it is to call a Christian a Jew.

sion, but no revelation of faith, doctrine, or morals is made except through the president. Mormons have a strong missionary imperative to convert the entire world because they believe that only through Mormonism can anyone attain full salvation.

Doctrine and Practice

Mormon teaching is based on four basic writings, collectively called the Standard Works: the Holy Bible (the King James Version in English-speaking countries), the *Book of Mormon*, the *Doctrine and Covenants* (revelations given to Joseph Smith and Brigham Young), and *The Pearl of Great Price*, an 1842 collection of allegedly ancient writings and those of Mormon contemporaries of Smith. These works have no fixed authority of their own, but are subject to ongoing interpretation and revision by church leaders, who are believed to receive continuing guidance and revelation from God.

Several Mormon doctrines are in sharp conflict with those of orthodox Christianity. Mormons are polytheistic and deny the doctrine of the Trinity as it is traditionally understood, teaching that the Trinity is constituted of three separate gods. The Father and Jesus Christ are physical persons, men who evolved into gods with a common purpose. "Latter-day Saints believe in God the Father; his Son, Jesus Christ; and the Holy Ghost. *These three Gods* form the Godhead, which holds the keys of power over the universe."[2] "The Father has a body of flesh and bones as tangible as man's; the Son also; but the Holy Ghost has not a body of flesh and bones, but is a personage of Spirit."[3] "[God] was once a man like us: [he] dwelt on earth, the same as Jesus Christ himself did."[4] "God himself was once as we are now, and is an exalted man, and sits enthroned in yonder heavens!"[5] Many Mormons believe that Jesus is the offspring of a sexual union between Mary and God the Father. Brigham Young maintained that the union was between Mary and the deified Adam, but this is no longer

2. Articles of Faith, Article 1 (italics mine).

3. *Doctrine & Covenants* 130:22.

4. *The Teachings of the Prophet Joseph Smith* (Salt Lake City, Utah: Deseret, 1977), pp. 345ff.

5. *The Teachings of the Prophet Joseph Smith*, p. 345.

taught.[6] Mormons also teach that Jesus was married — it was he who was the bridegroom at the wedding at Cana of Galilee.[7]

Mormons believe that all human souls preexisted and were conscious and accountable before becoming mortal human beings. Those who obey God's commandments and lead exemplarily righteous lives ultimately attain godhood after death. Only God, who is perfect, can be truly happy; therefore he rewards those who have loved and obeyed him by bestowing godhood on them. Although all Mormons will live in glory, only the truly righteous can achieve this godhood. While it is possible for non-Mormons to go to heaven, they cannot reach the highest spiritual states, including godhood. Since only Mormons can achieve these states, the question arises of the salvation of those who have gone before. Mormons believe that the dead will have an opportunity to accept the Mormon faith in the next life if they have not been exposed to it in this one. One can assist in the salvation of an ancestor through prayer, and be baptized for him as his proxy, as long as his name and lineage are known. Mormons have therefore developed extraordinary genealogical records. There is damnation and hell for evil people of any faith, including apostate Mormons.

Mormons deny the Nicene Creed, claiming that it is a corruption of the pure teachings of Jesus. Because of these divergences from orthodox teaching, Mormons refuse to participate in any ecumenical activity, including the National and World Councils of Churches. The more conservative Mormons will not worship with "Gentiles" (non-Mormons), although moderate and liberal ones will.

Worship is simple and only minimally liturgical, consisting of hymns, prayers, and preaching by laymen. A celebration of Holy Communion, which they refer to as "the Sacrament," is observed regularly on Sundays, using bread and water (wine is forbidden, and Mormons object even to the symbolic use of grape juice). Mormons worship in church-like meetinghouses and in homes in smaller communities. There are about two dozen temples around the world as well, in which laymen of "certified faithfulness" bless marriages and act as proxy for dead ancestors in order to bring them to salvation in the Mormon faith. The best-

6. Brigham Young, *Journal of Discourses* (Liverpool: F. D. Richards, 1854-55), pp. 50-51.

7. Young, *Journal of Discourses*, vol. 2, p. 80.

known of these is the Mormon Tabernacle in Salt Lake City, Utah. No non-Mormon is allowed to enter a temple beyond the outer court.

Mormons have many symbols, but they do not use the cross because they consider it idolatrous. Their most frequently used symbols are the beehive and the seagull. In obedience to a passage in Leviticus they took bees with them when they moved west (the beehive is now the state symbol of Utah). When they were first starting to farm in Utah they were attacked by a plague of locusts that threatened to destroy the crop and cause them to starve. A great flock of seagulls flew in and ate the locusts. This was seen as a miracle, since they were hundreds of miles inland.

A basic Mormon practice that bears a doctrinal mandate is extensive welfare work to the needy — Mormons "take care of their own," and there is no need for any Mormon ever to go on public welfare. They are also generous in helping non-Mormon needy. Stimulants and depressants are strictly forbidden, so alcohol, coffee, tea, and tobacco are banned. Many Mormons extend this even to caffeinated soft drinks. Education is highly valued by the church, which supports Brigham Young University in Provo, Utah, a school attended by over twenty-five thousand students. The religion organizes many youth activities, and Mormon troops of Boy Scouts and Girl Scouts are strongly supported in almost every larger community. Strong family bonds and the teaching of moral values are encouraged (as is witnessed by the many fine television spots sponsored by the Mormons).

Every young man over the age of sixteen who is "found worthy" (this includes most) is ordained to the priesthood, his preparation having started at age twelve. He is expected, if possible, to devote eighteen months to missionary work. The church maintains almost sixty thousand full-time missionaries. Until recently only white males could be ordained or speak officially for the church, and the role of blacks in the afterlife was ambiguous. In 1978 the prophet (president) had a revelation and declared that from then on blacks would have the same rights and privileges as whites. Women are still excluded from priesthood or any official role in the hierarchy, and it does not seem likely that this will change in the foreseeable future. Nevertheless, women are held in great respect, and Mormons are completely intolerant of any physical or emotional abuse of women or children. They will not baptize a married woman without the consent of her husband, or a minor without the consent of his parents. Although Mormons rely on the

Standard Works (see above) to learn about God, their basic knowledge of him is based on his revelations to Joseph Smith, to subsequent Mormon leaders, and to the prophet (the president of the church).

Structure and Hierarchy

Individual small congregations are called branches, larger ones wards, and both are staffed by lay members on a rotating basis. A ward's leadership consists of a bishop and two counselors, who serve terms of about five years. Activities of the ward, including worship and preaching, are shared by the members. There are no ordained clergy in the usual sense, although most young men are ordained priest. Above the ward is the stake, a collection of several wards, presided over by a three-man presidency and a high council of twelve. Collections of stakes are called regions, which are generally presided over by full-time leaders who rose to that position from the lower levels. While administrative decisions are made by the ward and stake leaders, policy, programs, and major decisions are centrally controlled. At the top administrative level are the presiding bishopric (consisting of a president and two counselors) and the first quorum of the seventy, with seven presidents. Above them is the central policy-making body, the council of the twelve apostles, and above them the first presidency, made up of the president (or prophet) and his two counselors. The president is looked on as being closer to God than others, and is a prophet of the status of Moses or Elijah; he is believed to attain godhood when he dies, assuming he has maintained the righteousness expected of this high office. All divine revelation is given through him and is indisputable — God protects him from making any serious error in faith and morals. (This is very close to the Roman Catholic doctrine of papal infallibility, which teaches that the pope, when he chooses to speak infallibly, can make no error on pronouncements of faith and morals.)

History

Mormonism was founded by Joseph Smith (1805-44). A member of a large, poor Vermont farming family, Smith grew up in Palmyra, New

York. At age fourteen he had a revelation in which God the Father and Jesus Christ visited him and told him that the true church was not to be found on earth. In 1827 he was visited by the Angel Moroni,[8] who led him to the buried *Book of Mormon*. According to Mormon teaching this was a collection of the writings of an ancient prophet named Mormon, a member of a tribe of Israelites who migrated to America in 600 BCE and carried their Jewish faith and culture with them. They split into two groups, the righteous Nephites and the corrupt and sinful Lamanites. After the resurrection Christ appeared to them, the Nephites accepted him, and he organized his church among them, but the Lamanites rejected him. In 385 CE, in a battle with the Lamanites, the Nephites were destroyed. Mormon, foreseeing this, recorded the entire history and teachings of the Nephites. Mormon's son Moroni abridged these writings and buried them, written on golden plates, in a drumlin at what is now Cumorah Hill outside Palmyra, New York. In 1827, resurrected as an angel, he led Smith to them and gave him a set of mystical tools by which he could translate them, called the *Urim* and *Thummim*.[9] The translation was completed in 1830.

Smith began to acquire followers, and just as quickly he gained enemies and persecutors. He and his followers moved west to Ohio and Missouri; persecution increased, fueled not only by religious prejudice and anger over the beginnings of polygamy, but also by economic fears resulting from the Mormons' rapidly growing numbers and strong unity. In spite of this persecution, converts were made at an astonishing rate. In 1844 Smith and his brother Hyrum were imprisoned in Carthage, Illinois, because of what were considered tyrannical and high-handed methods of dealing with apostates. There they were mur-

---

8. Moroni was human, the son of the prophet Mormon, and was resurrected to the status of an angel, a messenger of God. This contradicts Judeo-Christian theology, which teaches that humans do not become angels after death (despite the popular but erroneous mythology). Angels are a separate realm of creation — righteous humans are resurrected as saints. Mormonism has merged the separate Christian doctrines regarding angels and the communion of saints into a single construct.

9. *Urim* and *Thummim*, Hebrew for "Lights" and "Truths," were jewels on the breastplate of the high priest in ancient Judea. They were used for augury, probably by tossing them like dice. This was the justification for the apostles' "casting lots" to elect Matthias as a replacement for Judas (Acts 1:26).

dered by a mob. A power struggle ensued and over twenty splinter groups separated from the main body. In 1860 Smith's son, Joseph Smith III, accepted leadership of the largest of these. He established the Reorganized Church of Jesus Christ of Latter Day (instead of Latter-day) Saints. He forbade polygamy and organized a hierarchy of authority, being acknowledged as the prophet. Today that group is headquartered at Independence, Missouri, and has about half a million members. They also call themselves Mormons. In the meantime the majority of the original church was led by a group known as the Quorum of the Twelve Apostles. The president of the Quorum, Brigham Young, led them west until in 1847 they settled in the wilderness on the edge of the Great Salt Lake in Utah, where they established Salt Lake City. It was there that Young was acknowledged as President and Prophet of the church, with all the authority that had previously been held by Joseph Smith. The Mormons still faced persecution along with the hardships of surviving in the hostile environment and harsh climate of the Great Basin, but they nevertheless developed a prosperous society and strong church. Polygamy, though practiced by only about 15 percent of the Mormons, engendered many enemies, and was finally abolished in 1890. Mormonism had fairly well entered the mainstream of American culture by the turn of the century.

The Church of Jesus Christ of Latter-day Saints is a vital, growing religion that finds itself in an amicable but uneasy relationship with its surrounding cultures. Many people think of it as a conservative or fundamentalist Protestant sect, but it is in fact one of the newest disparate members of the world family of religions.

BAHA'I

The Baha'i faith can be thought of as the ultimate in ecumenism. It was founded in 1863 by the Persian (Iranian) sage Mirza Hoseyn Ali Nuri (1817-92), who declared that he was a messenger sent by God to announce a new revelation to all mankind. He took the name Bahaullah[1] ("Splendor of Allah"), and his disciples came to be known as Baha'i,[2] "Followers of the Splendor." His teachings were an amalgamation of those of all the major world religions, including Hinduism, Judaism, Zoroastrianism, Buddhism, Christianity, and Islam. They were strongly influenced by the teachings of 'Ali Mohammad of Shiraz ("The Bab"), an early nineteenth-century Persian reformer of Islam. Like most religious innovators, Bahaullah and his followers were persecuted for their beliefs and suffered torture, imprisonment, and exile. Bahaullah recorded his revelation in books, essays, and some fifteen thousand letters, all of which are now considered sacred scriptures of the faith. In these writings he addressed a vast spectrum of subjects, from the nature of spirituality to the role of music in childrearing. The writings are classified into four groups according to their four main kinds of subject matter: (1) the nature of God, (2) our relationship to God, (3) society and human relationships, and (4) the establishment of a Baha'i community.

1. Pronounced "ba-ha-OO-la."
2. Properly pronounced "ba-HA-ee," although commonly pronounced "ba-HIGH."

During the latter part of the nineteenth century Baha'ism spread from its birthplace in Iran throughout the Middle East, south into the Sudan, and into India. From there it spread across the Himalayas into Asia. Bahaullah appointed his son 'Abd ol-Baha (1844-1921) to be his successor as head of the Baha'i faith. 'Abd ol-Baha's name means "Servant of the Splendor." He wrote over twenty-seven thousand documents, mostly letters, which are also considered part of Baha'i sacred scripture. Under his leadership the faith spread throughout Europe, North America, South Africa, and Oceania. He was succeeded by Shoghi Effendi (1897-1957), Guardian of the Baha'i Faith from 1921 to 1957. Effendi oversaw the growth of the faith into Latin America and the rest of Africa. He laid the foundation for the election of the Universal House of Justice, which was first elected in 1963 and is the head institution of the Baha'i faith today. In 1991 the faith had about five million followers, with about 120,000 in the United States.

Teachings

Bahaullah defined God as "Unknowable Essence," teaching that he is so great that no matter how much we know of him there will always be vastly more that we are unable to comprehend. To enable us to know him at all he sends manifestations of himself in human form. These manifestations are very rare and will usually suffer for their teachings. Among them are Moses, Jesus, Buddha, Muhammad, and, of course, Bahaullah. Thus the Baha'i faith is simply the most recent of God's revelations.

Baha'ism teaches that God created the world, and that everything in it reflects some attribute of God. The human soul is immortal and contains all of God's attributes, but these cannot be manifested until they are developed. Spiritual development is the responsibility of the individual; there is no devil to hinder it, and no external force that saves us by relieving us of the responsibility of our failings. Success in that development is heaven, and failure is hell. Bahaullah stressed the importance of an active spiritual life based on daily study of sacred writings and regular prayer. There are three mandatory prayers for each day, and hundreds of prayers for all occasions. There is also an annual fasting period.

Bahaullah emphasized social responsibility and human equality, rejecting all racism, ethnicism, and social classes. There is a conscious effort to diversify the Baha'i community by attracting individuals from all races, nationalities, and stations in life. One's first responsibility is to the family of man, and only after that to one's nation. Baha'i advocates a single worldwide federal system of government to maintain peace and social justice. Baha'is do not believe that peace and justice can be enforced by government, only supported by it. Mankind's attitudes and values must first be changed. To exemplify these changes, Baha'is have formed a religious community dedicated to living by these standards.

Structure

Bahaullah envisioned a truly democratic and eclectic religious philosophy, in which every member would be consulted about his religious ideas, and from these thoughts a syncretism of all views could be achieved. All decisions about theology, practice, and discipline would be made only after discussion and consensus. There are no clergy — leadership is by an elected group. Each Baha'i community (which consists of all the Baha'is in an area) annually elects a nine-member spiritual assembly. This assembly assumes ownership of all property, organizes and oversees all spiritual activities (including marriages and funerals), and runs all secular programs such as schools or community centers. As far as possible all members are consulted before any controversial decisions are made. Similarly, a nine-member annually-elected national spiritual assembly runs all affairs of the religion on the national level, such as publishing, promoting educational materials and activities, and coordinating plans for expansion and international consolidation.

On the world level, activities are directed by the Universal House of Justice. This also has nine members who are elected for five-year terms by delegates elected by the national assemblies. The Universal House of Justice appoints counselors, who appoint auxiliary board members responsible for assisting and counseling the local assemblies. Through this system very efficient lines of communication are maintained between all levels of authority in the structure.

Faith and Practice

A Baha'i community consists of all people in a region who have accepted Bahaullah as the manifestation of God for this era. There is very little ritual in Baha'i worship. Nine holy days are observed during the year, but these are not particularly liturgical; they are, rather, times for the communities to meet and share their Baha'i commitment together. These holy days commemorate events in the lives of the Bab and Bahaullah. The Baha'i month consists of nineteen days, and once each Baha'i month the community observes what it calls a feast. This consists of study of scriptures, prayer, a business portion, and a social portion. On a weekly or monthly basis local Baha'i communities gather for prayer meetings, study, or "firesides" (home meetings for newcomers where the Baha'i teachings are presented at an introductory level). The Baha'i community operates over thirteen hundred social and economic development projects worldwide, including approximately 650 schools and seven radio stations. The United States has about 7,200 Baha'i communities, and 1,350 local spiritual assemblies. The Baha'i faith's national headquarters is near the Baha'i House of Worship in Wilmette, Illinois.

JEHOVAH'S WITNESSES

The Jehovah's Witnesses, although boasting millions of followers worldwide, would be better referred to as a cult than as a religious movement.[1] Their concept of God is essentially a reiteration of the Arian heresy[2] that was quelled by the church in the fourth century but has been resurrected every few generations since. In fact, among the heroes of Charles Taze Russell, the founder of the Jehovah's Witnesses, was the heretical Greek priest Arius himself. My analysis of the Jehovah's Witnesses is not quite as objective as that of the other faith groups, and I make no apology for that fact. My disapproval is based not on their beliefs, but on what I perceive to be their abuse of their adherents for the personal gain of a handful of members.

Doctrine and Practice

Jehovah's Witnesses believe that God has only one name, Jehovah,[3] and that all world religions, including Christianity, are the works

1. In fact, they deny being a religion, teaching that all worldly religions are Satan's work. For the criteria according to which I am classifying religious groups as "cults," see the introduction to "The Major Benign Cults," p. 61.

2. This heresy was taught by Arius, a fourth century CE Greek priest. Arians are not to be confused with Aryans, a tribe of Caucasian barbarians who invaded India about 1500 BCE, and who were idolized by the Nazis.

3. In early written Hebrew there were no vowels. The name of God was writ-

of the Devil. They believe in "the Christian religion," but they reject "Christianity." (Jehovah's Witnesses base their teachings on the Christian Scriptures, but orthodox Christians would not consider Jehovah's Witnesses to be Christians.) The Jehovah's Witnesses believe that they possess the only true Christian knowledge, revealed to mankind through the divine authority of the Watch Tower Bible and Tract Society. Jehovah's Witnesses are the precursors sent by God to warn men of the coming of a "theocratic kingdom" of which only they will be a part. This kingdom will be ruled by Jehovah. Participation in any worship, even prayer, with "Gentiles" (non-Witnesses) is a grievous offense. All ordained clergy are considered agents of the Antichrist and are thus damned.[4]

Jehovah's Witnesses reject the Trinity as an unbiblical construct, believing instead that God rules all his creation as a single divine person, not in the Trinity of Father, Son, and Holy Spirit. The Holy Spirit is not divine or personal, but is God's active power, and is referred to as "it." Jehovah's Witnesses also reject the divinity of Christ. Christ is not God, but a creature, the first creation of God, who lived in heaven as a "spirit-being" before he appeared on earth. When Jesus died this spirit-being returned to heaven, and when Jesus appeared to be resurrected he was actually supplanted by a newly created spirit-being who dwells in the upper air with divine powers (not as God). Witnesses believe Jesus will return to lead the forces of righteousness against the forces of evil in the Battle of Armageddon, will be victorious, and will reign as absolute ruler of the earth for a thousand years, after which the theocratic kingdom will be instituted. This kingdom is two-tiered. Most righteous people will live forever on earth after it is restored to the state of pure paradise that was found in Eden. An elect of 144,000

---

ten JHVH, believed to have been pronounced "Yahweh." The name was so sacred that it was not to be pronounced except by the high priest. When the Scriptures were read the reader said *Adonai*, "Lord." When vowel symbols were added to the text the vowels of Adonai were added to the name JHVH. This produced a word that is virtually unpronounceable in Hebrew so that God's name would not be accidentally spoken. Early translators, not understanding this, did the best they could and came up with *Jehovah*. In the Old Testament, "Lord" written in small capitals indicates where the name JHVH was used in the original Hebrew.

4. Yet Jehovah's Witnesses seek exemption from military service on the grounds that all Jehovah's Witnesses are "ministers of religion."

will enter heaven and dwell with God. There is no hell or eternal damnation, so at death sinners will simply be obliterated and cease to exist in any form. Total loyalty to this theocracy is demanded, so Witnesses may not take part in any activity that recognizes an existing government. (For example, not only military service, but even saluting the flag, are forbidden.) They do not recognize any religious or secular holidays — religious because they are pagan and satanic, and secular because they are the works of governments. While they do celebrate the resurrection of Jesus, they are careful not to confuse this with a celebration of Easter, which they maintain is based on pagan customs. They believe the Christian interpretation of the resurrection to be corrupt and false. It must be said to their credit that they are totally nondiscriminatory in matters of race or ethnicity.

Witnesses believe that Jesus was crucified on an upright stake and not on a cross. They therefore shun the cross both as an inaccuracy and as the symbol of a pagan religion (orthodox Christianity). They meet in buildings called "kingdom halls." These used to have a modified castle-like architecture, symbolic of the Watch Tower, but today they are usually simple rectangular structures.

Jehovah's Witnesses have a strict code of moral conduct, forbidding divorce except for the reason of adultery, and they are required to tithe. Based on biblical proscriptions they forbid any blood transfusion. Voluntary acceptance of a transfusion is a sin that will cause eternal extinction. Members of a local congregation or "company" are called "kingdom publishers." They are expected to spend at least five hours each week at kingdom hall, and as much time as possible in door-to-door preaching. "Pioneer publishers" work part-time and devote 100 hours per month to religious service, and "special pioneers" are salaried and spend at least 150 hours per month. Each kingdom hall has an assigned territory, and each "publisher" a designated neighborhood. They attempt to keep accurate records of all calls and contacts. The ultimate authority is the Watch Tower Bible and Tract Society, founded in 1884 and headquartered in Brooklyn, New York. (The headquarters of their publishing branch is in Pennsylvania.) The Watch Tower Society is the funnel through which God passes all revelation, and its authority in interpretation of Scripture and promulgation of doctrine and discipline is not to be questioned. All publications are written anonymously, and nothing is published without the Watch Tower's approval.

The History of the Witnesses

The cult was founded in 1872 by the son of a wealthy Pittsburgh draper, Charles Taze Russell (1852-1916). At the age of seventeen he tried unsuccessfully to convert an atheist, who in turn destroyed Russell's faith. At the age of twenty, having renounced both the Presbyterian and Congregationalist denominations, Russell fell in with some Adventists who convinced him that the Bible could be used to predict God's plan of salvation and the final conflict of good and evil ("the Battle of Armageddon"). He sold the haberdashery business he had inherited and formed a Bible class. Calling himself "Pastor Russell," he started by preaching what he called Millennial Dawn, that Christ would return to earth in 1874 to begin the final conflict. He was very much steeped in the occult and made this prediction based on the measurements of the Great Pyramid of Giza.[5] When this prediction failed to come to pass he announced in his tract *Thy Kingdom Come* that Christ had returned to earth "invisibly" in 1874, and that the great conflict and the end of the world would begin in 1914.[6] (In the 1916 edition he reported a different pyramid measurement proving that the invisible return had occurred in 1914.)

In 1884 he changed the name of his group to The Watch Tower Bible and Tract Society, and in 1879 started a Bible Journal called *The Watchtower*, which is still published. In 1919 he established a magazine called *The Golden Age*. This became *Consolation* in 1937 and in 1946 became *Awake!*, the name under which it is currently published. He published seven volumes of his own writings as *Studies in the Scriptures*. Today the Watch Tower Society is a flourishing publishing business reaching millions of people around the world.

Russell died suddenly in 1916. He is rarely mentioned by today's Witnesses, as he is something of an embarrassment to them for a number of reasons. His wife divorced him in 1897 on grounds of adultery, and to avoid the court-ordered alimony he transferred all his property to the Watch Tower Society. This was about $240,000, a huge fortune in

---

5. Pyramids play an important role in occultist thinking, and Russell attributed many mystical properties to them. His fascination with them is witnessed by his pyramid-shaped tomb.

6. "Thy Kingdom Come, Series III," p. 342, 1897 edition.

those days. He was shown many times to have been less than honest, including his 1913 sale of a miraculous cure for "surface cancer" and his marketing of "Miracle Wheat" that ended up in the courts on a fraud charge. He claimed to have mastered Latin, Greek, and Hebrew in order to study the Scriptures, but under oath in court in Hamilton, Ontario, in 1913 he admitted that he had no familiarity with any of these languages, and did not even know the Greek alphabet.

Upon Russell's death the group was led for a while by the Board of Directors as a committee, without a designated leader. In 1918 leadership was taken by "Judge" Joseph Franklin Rutherford (1869-1942). In 1892, seeing the potential of the Watch Tower Society, he became a lawyer and joined the society as their attorney. He went to prison for sedition in 1916 because he refused to do military service in World War I,[7] and took control of the organization upon his release after the war. His title of "Judge" was self-appointed. It was he who established the slogan "Millions now living will never die," and with it brought enormous crowds to hear his message. During his time as leader he expanded the Watch Tower Bible and Tract Society into a huge publishing empire. In 1931 he renamed the movement "Jehovah's Witnesses." He died in 1942 in his palatial villa in San Diego.

Rutherford was succeeded in 1942 by Nathan Homer Knorr (1905-77), whose major contributions were the establishment of a missionary training school and the production of a new translation of the Bible. Under him membership grew from 155,000 to over 2.5 million. He was succeeded by Frederick W. Franz (1893-1992), a charismatic leader who, like Russell, claimed to be a master of classical languages and a Rhodes Scholar. In fact he had taken only introductory courses in Latin and classical (not biblical) Greek before dropping out of college in his junior year. The closest he came to a Rhodes Scholarship was taking a qualification test for it (the record of his score is lost, but he was not awarded the scholarship). He was reputedly an alcoholic, and vehemently opposed Prohibition, which in a 1924 Watchtower article he designated "a scheme of the devil." He died in 1992 at the age of ninety-nine, at which time the current president, Milton G. Henschel (1921-), took office.

---

7. Had he claimed conscientious objector status, he would have been allowed alternative service; he was imprisoned because he would not acknowledge the United States (or any political entity) as a lawful government.

The Jehovah's Witnesses are a fascinating cult, but they are a matter of great concern to orthodox Christians (as well as to the adherents of most other religions). In spite of major inconsistencies and outright chicanery, they somehow manage to get tremendous control over the lives of their believers. They hold a special appeal to the ignorant underclasses, whose exploitation produces immense power and wealth for the handful of men who control the Watch Tower Bible and Tract Society.

NEOPAGANISM

Wicca, Asatru, and Druidism

The term "pagan" is derived from the Latin *paganus*, "country dweller." Often used to refer to one who is neither Christian, Jew, nor Muslim, it more correctly refers to a follower of a polytheistic religion based on nature worship. There are hundreds of such religions practiced in the civilized world. Many are revivals of ancient practices, and are generally classified as "Neopaganism." Neopaganism is an attempt to reconnect with nature through the symbolism of the ancient religions, although some Neopagans go beyond symbolism and believe literally in the deities they worship.[1] Neopagan religions are particularly attractive to many of the people who are deeply involved in the various "Earth first" movements. Among the most widespread of the Neopagan religions are Wicca (Witchcraft), Asatru (the worship of the Teutonic gods of the Aesir), and Druidism (the religion of the ancient Celts). These three religions have many beliefs and practices in common. Followers of all three worship nature, delve into the occult, and practice magic. They also share as holy the same cycles of the liturgical year. The two solstices, the two equinoxes (the midpoints between each), and the thirteen lunar cycles are times of special ceremonies in each religion.

---

1. Even in ancient times many of the adherents of the pagan religions, such as those of Greece and Rome, believed more in the symbolism of the mythology than in a literal interpretation. On the other hand, many accepted the stories as fact.

Wicca

"Wicca" (Old English for "sorcerer") is a revival of an early pagan religion based on astrology, magic, the occult, and a variety of polytheistic traditions. It is rooted in ancient occultism, but its revival was popularized in the middle of this century by the English writer Gerald Gardner in his book *Witchcraft Today* (1954), in which he explored the religions of ancient Britain. It spread to America in the 1960s, in part because of its popularity with feminists who were seeking an earth-based female-oriented religion. There is a wide spectrum of deities worshiped by various Wiccan groups, but most focus on the Great Goddess (similar to the ancient earth goddess Gaia) and her horned consort, the god of nature and fertility (in Greek mythology the god Pan). The image of Pan, with his horns and goat's feet, has contributed to the unfounded accusation that Wiccans are devil-worshipers.

Wiccan ritual uses many ceremonial items, the most common being a ritual knife and a chalice. Other ritual items which have encouraged much of the prejudice and misunderstanding about Wicca include bells, brooms, candles, cauldrons, drums, pentacles, herbs, and wands. Most rituals begin with creating a "sacred space" by casting a circle or pentacle (five-pointed star). There is the invocation of divine or spiritual power, dancing, incantations, and often food. Poetry and creative literature are highly regarded in Wicca and play an important part in the rituals — many of the Wiccans' sacred incantations are in rhyme.[2] There are rituals for such occasions as weddings, births, and funerals. Ancient prejudice accuses Wiccans of trafficking with and even worshiping Satan, but this is a false charge. Many rituals take place at night. There is also magic and spell-casting, so it is obvious how prejudice and ignorance would lead to accusations of evil practice.[3]

In early Christian times Wiccans were often viewed favorably because they were believed to have special beneficial powers and knowledge of healing and good luck (the so-called "white witches"). About the time of the First Crusade (1095 CE) the tide turned and "the burn-

2. Shakespeare played on this in *Macbeth* when he had the "three sisters" chant, "Double, double, toil and trouble, fire burn and cauldron bubble."

3. There are many Satanic cults in existence, and there have been for millennia. Wicca and its predecessors, however, cannot be fairly accused of Satanic worship or practice.

ing time" began. In the course of the next six centuries tens of thousands of men, women, and children (but mostly women) were burned or hanged for witchcraft all over Europe. The last of the great pogroms of witches took place in 1692 in Salem, Massachusetts, when several hundred "witches" were imprisoned and twenty executed.[4]

Many Wiccans call themselves witches, yet they often deny that Wicca and Witchcraft are the same thing. In essence, however, they are. The reason for the denial is obvious — the term "witch" conjures up a variety of eerie images from a green-faced hag riding on a besom to *Macbeth*'s "three sisters" hovering over the bubbling cauldron. Wiccans are not malevolent or dangerous. They have a religion that by modern Western standards may seem strange and perhaps quaint, but it is neither a joke nor a cult. Theirs is not a proselytizing religion: they do not seek converts, and they resent attempts to convert them. Most people would not find their moral and ethical code offensive. It is based on the "Wiccan Rede," which is summed up in the ancient Wiccan equivalent of the Golden Rule, "An it harm none, do as thou wilt." Although somewhat libertarian by Christian standards, they consider this rule a major imperative in all human relationships.

Asatru

Asatru (pronounced "Ah-SAH-troo") is a revival of the worship of the Aesir and the Vanir,[5] the pre-Christian gods of northern Europe (including Odin, Frigg, and Thor). In many ways Asatru is similar to Wicca, which undoubtedly had an early influence on it. It is practiced

---

4. The traditional method of executing witches in Europe was burning at the stake. This was never practiced in America, however, where witches were hanged. In the Salem purge, nineteen individuals were hanged for witchcraft, and one, Giles Corey, was crushed to death for refusal to testify, accuse, or confess.

5. Aesir, pronounced "AY-seer," is the plural of the Old Norse *ase*, "god"; Vanir, pronounced "VAH-neer," is the plural of *vane*, "mighty one." The Aesir were the Norse gods, and the Vanir were another race of gods (possibly equivalent to the Mediterranean Titans) who lived with the Aesir in Asgard, the equivalent of Mount Olympus. The common misconception is that they lived in Valhalla, but this is incorrect. Valhalla was Odin's palace in Asgard, in the Great Hall of which heroes who fell in battle were honored.

worldwide, although the majority of its adherents are of northern European extraction. The name is an Old Norse word meaning "Faith in the Aesir," and its followers are known as Asatruar. As in most pagan religions, it is closely tied to nature and the earth. Its primary symbol is *Mjollnir*, Thor's hammer. (Thor was seen as the protector of the earth.) Estimates of Asatru's time of origin vary, but the main consensus puts it at about 1000 BCE. It is described in Tacitus's *Germania* (ca. 100 CE). Most of the lore of modern Asatru is derived from the thirteenth-century Icelandic *Edda*, heroic sagas that tell of Viking exploits and beliefs. Its revival began in Iceland in the 1970s under the leadership of the late Sveinbjorn Bentisson, a noted Icelandic poet. During the past quarter century it has spread throughout the world. Asatru is a state-recognized religion in Iceland and Norway and is recognized by the IRS in the United States as a tax-exempt religion.

According to Asatru belief, the universe consists of *Yggdrasil*, a great ash tree that binds together nine worlds, including Asgard, the home of the gods, and Midgard, the physical universe as we know it (including Earth). The gods include Odin or Wotan, the one-eyed creator of the universe and ruler of the gods,[6] and his wife Frigg or Fricka; Thor, his eldest son and protector of Midgard and god of war; Frey, god of the sun, rain, and the fruits of the earth, and his sister Freya, goddess of love; Sif, goddess of the harvest; Tyr, the one-armed goddess of justice (being one-armed, she cannot use a sword and shield at the same time — she must either prosecute or defend, but not both at once); and Loki, god of discord and evil, and disrupter of Asgard. There are also Valkyries, dragons, fairies, and a host of lesser spiritual beings. Some adherents seem to take these beliefs literally, but most consider them symbolic of higher spiritual and moral values.[7]

6. Odin traded an eye for a magic spear by which he could find power and wisdom. He keeps two ravens, Hugin and Munin, who fly across the whole world every day and then return to him in the evening to report all they have seen. His pets are two wolves who always travel with him, and to whom he gives all solid food that is set before him. His sole nourishment is mead (fermented honey).

7. These gods all have Mediterranean equivalents: Odin = Kronos; Frigg = Rhea (Kronos's sister and wife); Thor = Zeus (Jupiter) and his son Ares (Mars); Frey = Helios (Apollo); Freya = Aphrodite (Venus); Sif = Hera, Zeus's sister and wife (Juno), and also Demeter (Ceres); Tyr = Justitia; and Loki = Eris (Discordia). The Nordic gods provided the names for Tuesday (Tyr's Day), Wednesday (Wotan's Day), Thursday (Thor's Day), and Friday (Frey's Day).

Many Asatruar are also fascinated with the social customs of their ancestors, reenacting Viking activities such as sword fighting and divining.[8] The primary values embraced by Asatru are wisdom, strength, courage, joy, honor, freedom, vigor, and the importance of ancestry. Being pagan and thus nature-oriented, Asatru worship is based on the changing of the seasons; other fixed festivals are observed, but these, too, are based on themes of nature. Worship practices are intended to follow as closely as possible those of the Viking days, with the exception that at the *Blot* (blood ceremony) mead (honey wine) is usually used in place of animal sacrifice. A *Blot* is a formal ritual to honor a particular deity. Another common rite is the *Sumbel*, which is performed after dark. A circle is formed around a fire, and a boast, toast, curse, or saga is told. This is followed by a ceremonial drink of mead. No food is used, as Odin's sole nourishment is mead. There are also wedding rites, "name-givings" for children, and funeral ceremonies. There is no prayer — communication with the gods is in conversational form. The gods are not seen as masters, so there is no bowing or subservience to them. They are powerful kinfolk rather than superiors.

It is sometimes difficult for us in the twenty-first century to envision others taking a religion such as Asatru seriously, but we must recognize that many do. The faith undoubtedly attracts a range of believers, from serious votaries to those who are almost playing at it, but the same range can be found in Christianity. Despite the ferocity of the Vikings, the Norsemen were not a horde of unwashed barbarians. They were in many respects a highly civilized people. The followers of Asatru realize this and are attempting to distill the best of Nordic culture into their faith.

---

8. It must be said in defense of the early Norsemen that they were not ignorant barbarians. The Vikings, who were the Norse military, were cruel, fierce, merciless warriors. The British and Celts, whose writings left us with the modern image of the Vikings, were victims of their raids for over three centuries. They understandably saw them as a base and vicious people. In fact, the Norse civilization produced beautiful works of art, advanced technology, the first true democracy in Europe, and a richly imaginative and poetic legendry.

Druidism

Druidism arose in the mists of prehistory in the practices of sorcery and shamanism. Like Wicca and Asatru, it is strongly nature-oriented, its primary symbol being the oak tree. Druidism was practiced all across the European continent in prehistoric times, but it eventually became concentrated among the nomadic Celtic tribes as they moved west across central Europe. As they moved into the British Isles and slowly disappeared from the continent, so did Druidism.[9] By the time the Romans had conquered most of Europe, the Celts and their religion were firmly ensconced in Britain and on the Brittany coast. The first reliable description we have of Druidism is in Roman accounts of British culture written in the time of the Emperor Claudius.

As a polytheistic pagan faith Druidism was inconsistent with Christianity, and the early Christians worked hard to suppress it. Most of the stories of Druids practicing cruel and bloodthirsty human sacrifice were promulgated by Christian propagandists.[10] Druidism as it is practiced today is the revival of that very ancient form of nature-worship, and has accommodated itself well to modern culture. Druidism is not a violent religion, but a peaceful one that practices meditation and reflection. It also espouses the same rule as Wicca, that the guide to all action is to do no harm (even to oneself). Druids believe that the earth is actually a single living being pervaded by gods and spirits of all kinds, a being of which we are but a small part. Druidism is thus pantheistic, worshiping gods in all aspects of nature. Its followers believe that short of harming the earth or other people there is no sin, and that there is no evil spirit such as Satan. They maintain that the gods are strong enough to defend their own honor and cannot be hurt by mankind, so there is no such thing as blasphemy or heresy. Druidic worship is very similar to that of Wicca and Asatru, except that there is less emulation of ancient rituals. Wor-

9. The continental Celts did not really disappear, but diversified and were absorbed into other barbarian tribes, becoming less identifiable as a unique people. The Gauls that Caesar fought were mainly Celts, not Frenchmen. Similarly, the "Franks" of the Holy Roman Empire were also not French, but Celtic Germans.

10. There is evidence that Druids did occasionally practice human sacrifice, and that the victims volunteered for it. Most Druidic sacrifice, however, was of an animal, the flesh of which was then used to feed the village.

shipers meet in small groups called "groves" for the purpose of discussion, meditation, and study.

There are countless other pagan religions practiced today throughout the world by peoples ranging from poverty-stricken Amazon Valley Indians to wealthy urban sophisticates. Some educated and civilized pagans are "playing religion" and relishing being different; some are grasping to satisfy a spiritual hunger that the church has failed to fill; but we must remember that although this faith system is quite foreign to ours, some individuals are devout believers in it and sincere worshipers, and must be respected as such.

UNITARIAN-UNIVERSALISM

Freethinkers are not followers of a religion, but rather are believers in the total intellectual independence of the individual. While they cannot really be classified into any one group, many (but certainly not all) would qualify as atheists[1] or agnostics.[2] The American Heritage Dictionary defines a freethinker as "One who has rejected authority and dogma, especially in religious thinking, in favor of rational inquiry and speculation." This does not require the rejection of religion, but simply the refusal to accept the authority of religion over that of the conscience or reason of the individual. Peter Abelard and (before he recanted) Galileo certainly qualified as freethinkers, yet they were by no means atheists, and they never questioned the authority of God or

1. Many atheists like to claim that any freethinker is atheistic — for example, they identify Thomas Jefferson as an atheist. Jefferson was one of the greatest of the freethinkers, but he was not an atheist. There is little question that he was a Deist. Deism was a popular eighteenth-century philosophy which essentially taught that God exists, that he created the universe and pervades it, but that he does not interfere with or influence its operation. Deists believed, however, that mankind was obligated to live by the principles that God incorporated into his creation. Thus Jefferson could in good conscience support the motto of the United States, "In God we trust."

2. An agnostic is "a person who holds the view that any ultimate reality (as God) is unknown and probably unknowable," or, more broadly, "one who is not committed to believing in either the existence or the nonexistence of God or a god" (Merriam-Webster's Collegiate Dictionary, tenth edition). The term "agnosticism" comes from the Greek for "unknown."

the validity of the Roman Catholic Church. They simply denied that any individual or group had authority over the ideas and conscience of another. In essence, freethinkers defend the right to be wrong.

The Unitarian-Universalist Association is not a religion but a society of freethinkers — in fact, it is the largest organization of freethinkers in America. Notwithstanding, we will consider it in this book because most people, including many of its members, think of it as a religious group, and it did begin as one. It has roots in Judaism and Christianity, and yet does not profess a belief in or denial of any god. One is free to believe almost anything one wants and yet be a member of this society, which embraces the entire spectrum of thought from atheism to total commitment to a deity. Today most UUs (as Unitarian-Universalists refer to themselves) believe at most that there is an impersonal power or force in the universe, which they often refer to as "it" rather than as "he."

UUs place an almost obsessive value on intellect and freedom of thought (the radio commentator Brad Crandall described them as "an intellectual ghetto"). Most UU groups meet on Sunday morning, not for any religious reason, but simply for the sake of tradition and because it seems to be a convenient time for most members. There is no standardized or traditional liturgy. The structure and content of the meeting is determined entirely by the will of the local congregation. There is rarely any prayer at their meetings, and the word "God" is seldom mentioned. They observe Easter and Christmas, but purely as seasons symbolic of human goodwill, attributing no religious significance to either holiday. Most believe in the validity of Jesus' moral and social teachings, even though many maintain that Jesus, like King Arthur, is a legendary character based on some historic individual.

This nonreligious (almost anti-religious) attitude is relatively new. Unitarianism goes back to the earliest days of the Protestant Reformation in Europe, although it did not identify itself as a unique religious philosophy until its formal organization in Transylvania in 1825. Universalism, although based on an ancient concept of salvation for every human (the doctrine of universal salvation), was formally organized in 1793. It was in 1961 that the two groups merged as the Unitarian-Universalist Association (UUA), at which time they affirmed themselves as being neither Christian nor theistic. I was raised in the Unitarian Church in the 1930s and '40s (yes, they called it a church then), before the merger with the Universalists. The Sunday service was based on Bible reading and prayer, and was definitely theological and Christ-oriented, even though the doctrine of the Trinity was rejected. The typical service, in fact, was very similar to the Anglican service of Morning Prayer. Most members in those days identified themselves as Christians, though they were ultra-liberal in their theology. The only creed at that time was unofficial but generally accepted: "I believe in the fatherhood of God, the brotherhood of man, and the leadership of Jesus."[3] Today the only tenet of that creed that would be universally accepted in the movement is "the brotherhood of man," although in this politically-correct era it is generally expressed as "the family of humankind." For most of its history Unitarian theology was similar to that of the liberal end of Reform Judaism — in fact, Unitarians were often described as Jews without the Judaic racial or cultural heritage. Some congregations observed rites paralleling Christian rites, such as an initiation rite for infants similar to baptism, and a confirmation-like welcoming into the congregation. Most had a ceremony of mutual commitment for marriage, and funeral rites of remembrance. Theology and practice are both drastically different since the merger.

There are a little over a thousand UUA congregations in North America, and a handful of UU groups in other regions around the world that are not officially part of the UUA. All UU congregations are self-governing. In most congregations there is a governing board elected from the membership. Each congregation determines its own requirements for its ministers, although most expect an academic degree from a university or theological seminary and recognition from the UUA. There is no ordination in the traditional sense, although there is a ceremony for the recognition of ministry. Congregational activities include such things as Sunday school, day-care centers, lectures and forums, support groups, poetry festivals, drama, family events, adult-education classes, and study groups. Congregations are totally freethinking, in that members may believe whatever they wish and still be recognized as members in good standing. Some congregations, however, have a distinct theological position, although no indi-

---

3. To which some wit added, "And the neighborhood of Boston." This is not wholly inappropriate, since Boston is one of the strongest UU centers in America, and the national headquarters are there.

vidual member is required to accept it. For example, in the 1970s and '80s the Rust Street Universalist Church in Salem, Massachusetts, affirmed the doctrine of the Trinity, and Christian theology (albeit very liberal) was often taught there from the pulpit.

The UUA has no legislative authority, but simply serves as a central provider of resources to its independent member congregations. It provides study materials, consultations, and support; institutes social action programs; and disseminates information and news through a bimonthly magazine, *The World*. It maintains The Beacon Press, a publishing house that specializes in theologically, socially, and politically liberal pamphlets and books. The UUA works alongside many worldwide religious and secular organizations to provide a wide range of social services.

THE MAJOR BENIGN CULTS

The Unification Church and Hare Krishna

The term "cult" commonly refers to a religious or pseudo-religious group that espouses a set of beliefs that is severely disparate from the mainstream culture; generally such a group also accepts total submission to the teachings of a charismatic leader or founder. Many belief systems might be considered cults at their outset, but are justified by their survival over long periods of time. Most major world religions have met this criterion.

Most cults are benign, meaning that they do no particular spiritual, physical, moral, or financial damage to their members or to others. Some, on the other hand, are dangerous — Heaven's Gate was a suicide cult, the Charles Manson Family were murderers, and Jim Jones's People's Temple was responsible for both murder and suicide. There are others that do great psychological harm or brainwash their members into giving all their worldly possessions to the leaders.

Two of the major cults that have been accused of many harmful acts can be found, under examination, to be relatively benign. They are the Unification church of the Reverend Sun Myung Moon and the Hare Krishna movement.[1]

1. In June, 2000, a lawsuit was initiated against ISKCON (Hare Krishna), alleging physical, mental, and sexual child abuse in ISKCON boarding schools in the 1970s. Officials of ISKCON admit that some abuse may have taken place, but claim that when it was discovered it was immediately stopped, the perpetrators punished, and all ISKCON boarding schools closed and converted to day schools in order to avoid a repetition in the future. This suit will probably go on for a long time,

THE UNIFICATION CHURCH

History

"The Holy Spirit Association for the Unification of World Christianity" was founded in 1954 in Seoul, Korea, by Young Oon Kim, an engineer, who now calls himself the Reverend Sun Myung Moon ("One Who Has Clarified the Truth"). His followers are called "Moonies" by outsiders, but they consider this irreverent, preferring to be called "Unificationists." Moon was born in 1920 in what is now North Korea and was raised a Presbyterian. He claims to have had a vision at age fifteen, in which Jesus commanded him to complete the work that Jesus had started. Moon had several run-ins with the law in Korea and later in the United States. In 1948 he was excommunicated for heresy by the Korean Presbyterian Church. In 1957 he published a collection of his beliefs, entitled *Divine Principle.* He came to North America in 1959 to seek converts and was phenomenally successful. His timing was perfect, as this was the period of the rebellion of the younger generation that produced the "hippies" and fed dozens of new cults. In 1982 he instituted the practice of mass weddings, in the first of which two thousand couples were married in a single ceremony. In 1984 Moon was sentenced to thirteen months in prison for tax evasion. Addicted to drugs, he was admitted to the Betty Ford Clinic, but he failed to complete the program.

Moon is the final authority in all church matters; the administration of the church's religious and business activities is by a board of elders appointed by and responsible to him. He had identified his son Hyo Jin Moon as his heir as ruler of the church, but several scandals surrounding his children have left him without a designated heir. The Unification church is active all over the world, although its membership reports have been shown to be grossly inflated. It is involved in hundreds of political, cultural, and business operations, most of which have proven to be extremely profitable.

---

but it merits watching. One question in defense of ISKCON is why it took over twenty-five years for this charge to surface.

Beliefs and Practices

Followers of the cult believe that God is a single, perfect being, and reject the Trinity. The Holy Spirit is a feminine counterpart to God. She is a form of energy, not a person. Before Adam and Eve were married in Eden, Eve had a sexual affair with the Archangel Lucifer, causing the spiritual fall of mankind; she then had a premarital sexual affair with Adam, causing the physical fall. This destroyed the unity of the family, thus allowing Satan to control the world. Jesus was born of a sexual union between Mary and Zechariah, but he was free of original sin; he died and was spiritually resurrected, although his physical body remained in the grave. God's plan for Jesus, who was the Second Adam, was for him to have a perfect marriage, thus restoring the unity of the family and driving Satan out. Since he was executed before this could happen, it will be up to a Third Adam to complete this work. This Adam was to be born in Korea between 1917 and 1930. Moon does not claim to be the Third Adam, but when his followers identify him and his second wife, Hak Ja Han, as such, he does not deny it. The stated mission of the Unification church is to unite all Christians into one church.

The Unification church is very family-centered. Members must remain celibate while young and eventually must marry. Marriages are arranged by the church a month in advance, but couples are allowed to refuse without disgrace. A "Pledge Service" is held at 5:00 a.m. each Sunday, on the first day of each month, and on January first. There are five annual celebrations: God's Day, Parents' Day, Children's Day, The Day of All Things, and True Parent's Birthday (the birthday of Sun Myung Moon).

Many of the accusations of the cult's opponents are unfair, although they merit attention. There is unquestionably considerable mind control of the most committed members, but the accusations of imprisonment and forced brainwashing are false. Until members reach a deep stage of commitment they are free to leave the cult without serious harassment or threat; it is extremely difficult and possibly dangerous, however, for inner-core members to defect. Most who do suffer severe psychological problems, including depression, self-accusation, and paranoid behavior.

There is no indication that this is a self-destructive cult such as the

People's Temple or Heaven's Gate. During the 1960s and '70s, many members were kidnapped by family members and "deprogrammed" in an attempt to destroy their allegiance to the cult. Although illegal, this is still done today, but it is relatively rare.

HARE KRISHNA

History

The cult commonly called "Hare Krishna" is properly known as ISKCON, an acronym for "International Society for Krishna Consciousness." It is based on the Vaishna Hindu culture, the ancient Hindu worship of the god Krishna ("the Exalted One"). *Hare* (pronounced "HAH-ray") is equivalent to the Sanskrit for "hail." ISKCON was founded in 1966 by a disciple of the Hindu guru Caitanya, Abhay Charan De, who adopted the name Bhaktivedanta Swamiji Prabhupada (*swamiji* means "beloved teacher"), but is usually referred to as Srila Prabhupada ("Most Honorable Master"). He was born in Calcutta in 1896. In 1922 his spiritual master Srila Thakur charged him to preach the word of Krishna in English. He took this charge to heart, but did not act on it for several years while he built a successful pharmaceutical business in Calcutta. He began preaching part-time in 1936, and in 1944 began publishing the magazine *Back to Godhead.* In 1950 he left his home, family, and business to preach full-time, and in 1959 took the vow of *sanyasa,* complete renunciation of material things. He started writing what would become fifty volumes of spiritual literature.

In 1962 he begged passage on a tramp steamer and came to America, where he settled in New York's lower east side. There he amassed a large number of followers of all social classes. His most dedicated disciples took the habit of Hindu monks, shaving their heads and wearing saffron robes. One day he took his disciples to Tompkins Park, where they began a *sankirtan,* a chanting session. This drew large crowds of curious onlookers. Subsequent *sankirtans* resulted in many new disciples, mainly young people who felt abandoned by society and were seeking some form of spiritual satisfaction. (Such individuals were plentiful in the turbulent 1960s.) In 1966 he incorporated ISKCON and developed the infrastructure for worldwide proselytizing. He went to San Francisco to develop a branch of ISKCON there, and found it to be particularly attractive to the large communities of hippies on the West Coast. By the time Srila Prabhupada died in 1977, ISKCON had become a worldwide movement.

Beliefs and Practices

Chanting is a major part of the discipline of the cult. The constantly repeated mantra is *Om, hare Krishna, hare Krishna, Krishna, Krishna, hare, hare, hare Rama, hare Rama, Rama, Rama, hare, hare, Om.* This is a hymn of praise to two of Brahma's avatars, Krishna and Rama, who represent the same premier god. *Om* is a sacred syllable in Hinduism (as well as in several other mystic traditions), representing the perfect essence of the universe. Hare Krishnas share many beliefs with conventional Hindus. Their sacred text is the Bhagavad-Gita, a poem containing conversations between Lord Krishna and a soldier. Their goal is to escape *samsara*, the endless cycle of repetitive reincarnations, and return to nirvana. Their main divergences from Hinduism are the worship of Krishna as the supreme god, and the teaching that they can attain enlightenment only through the descendants of the swami Caitanya.

There are two parts to ISKCON — a cloistered monastic order and lay members who live in ordinary homes. All clergy live a rigidly disciplined life, including strict vegetarianism. They spend several hours a day in prayer and *sankirtan* (chanting). Celibacy is required of all single members, and married members may use sexual activity solely for procreation. Many members of the congregation follow to some degree the disciplines of the monks, including vegetarianism, although this is not required. All food that is eaten is offered first as a sacrifice to Lord Krishna. Lay people may eat meat, but it must be killed mercifully.

Hare Krishnas became well-known in the 1960s and '70s because of their appearance in airports and other public places with shaven heads and saffron robes. They played Indian music, spoke softly, begged, gave away flowers, and sold their literature; because of their unusual appearance and manner of speech they frightened many people into thinking they must be dangerous. In 1992 the Supreme Court allowed the banning from public places of anyone soliciting money. Hare Krishnas make people of more traditional cultures very uncomfortable, but there is no evidence that their cult is dangerous either to its members or to others.

PART TWO

THE MANY FACES OF CHRISTIANITY

A BRIEF HISTORY
OF THE CHRISTIAN CHURCH

It is impossible to consider the denominations of the Christian church outside the context of history. They were formed as much by the events and politics of their times as by the theology of their founders. For example, it is unlikely that there would ever have been a break between the Roman Catholic and Eastern Orthodox Churches had there not also been a schism in the Roman Empire. Trying to write a history of the church in a few hundred words is rather like the assignment, "Describe the universe and give two other examples." Notwithstanding, we must at least examine the course of the church's life as schism has led to schism. The church can be pictured as a tree, with branch after branch growing off from the main stem. A couple of times a new shoot has been formed completely apart from the main plant, but based on the same root system.

A false modern myth is that the early church was stable, unified, and secure, and that a return to the practices of those times would ensure a revival of truly Christ-like principles. This is a lovely dream, but it is simply not true. Even in apostolic times the church was rife with disagreement, heresy, schism, and sometimes outright corruption. The first record of this is in the book of Acts, where a dispute is recorded between those who maintained that anyone could be a Christian and those who argued that one had to become a Jew before becoming a Christian (the "Judaizers"). There are also divisions of loyalty related in 1 Corinthians 1:10-17.

The first three centuries of the church are known as the age of persecution. In the Roman Empire religions had to be licensed. Judaism was legal, but when Christians began to see themselves as separate from Jews and the Jews rejected them, they were no longer accepted as members of a legal faith. Because of their illegitimate status and their prophecy that the world would end in fire, they were the obvious scapegoats for Nero when the people blamed him for the burning of Rome in 64 CE. This began a period of bloody persecutions, and persecutions would reoccur sporadically until 313, when the Emperor Constantine converted to Christianity and established it as the primary faith of the empire. In spite of the persecution, Christianity filled an increasing spiritual vacuum for the people and grew at an astonishing rate throughout the empire.

Toward the end of the third century a priest named Arius taught that Christ was a special creature of God, and not God himself. His teachings came to be known as Arianism, and gained huge numbers of followers, at one time including twice as many people as were orthodox Christians. At the Council of Nicaea in 325 CE, however, Arius's teachings were condemned as heresy, and the view, championed by Saint Athanasius, that Christ was of "one substance" with the Father was approved as the orthodox position. Neverthless, the influence of Arianism was felt for centuries, and its teachings can be found today in the theology of groups such as the Jehovah's Witnesses. Arianism was the first major heresy in the church (the rift with the Judaizers mentioned above was quickly healed).

During the next three centuries the Roman Empire not only declined, it effectively divided in two, with the Western empire centered in Rome[1] and the Byzantine Empire in Constantinople (now Istanbul, Turkey). As this split widened, distinct traditions and theological views developed that were unique to the Eastern and Western churches. The Byzantine Empire remained relatively strong, but a series of weak emperors and disastrous political, military, and theological events caused the slow death of the Western empire. As a result, the power of the church increased, and for the most part settled in the person of the bishop of Rome, the pope. By the beginning of the seventh

---

1. The sacking of Rome by the Vandals in 455 CE was not the end of the Roman Empire, but it certainly marked the end of its already badly eroded influence on the rest of the world.

century he was in effect the undisputed ruler of the West. Although it had no real connection to the classical Roman Empire, the region that had been the Western empire would become known as the Holy Roman Empire upon the crowning of Charlemagne as Emperor in 800 CE. During the feudal Middle Ages, the hundreds of tiny city-states throughout Europe had so little power that the church became a secular power, with the pope seen as a prince as well as a spiritual ruler.[2] While he had no secular authority over the Eastern lands, he nevertheless claimed that as Peter's successor he had full spiritual authority over all Christendom. The patriarch of Constantinople, averring spiritual descent from St. Paul, made a similar claim.

In the early seventh century Islam arose in Arabia, and with stunning speed swept westward through the Middle East, across North Africa, and into the Iberian Peninsula, virtually obliterating Christianity in those regions. (With the exception of Israel and Iberia, those lands are still predominantly Muslim to this day.) The advance slowed somewhat after the conquest of Spain, but it would not be completely checked until the Battle of Tours, France, in 732 CE. Islam was not driven from Iberia until El Cid's victory at Valencia in 1094 CE.

By the eleventh century the rift between the Eastern and Western churches had reached a point of no return, resulting in what is known as the Great Schism. In 1054 CE an emissary of the pope went to the Cathedral of the Holy Wisdom in Constantinople and laid on the high altar a bull of excommunication, declaring that the entire Eastern church was cast out and damned for heresy. In return the patriarch of Constantinople excommunicated the entire Western church. Although formal reconciliation efforts began in 1968, it is likely that the Eastern Orthodox and Roman Catholic Churches will remain separate for a long time to come.

In 1095 the pope organized the first Crusade to wrest the Holy Land from the control of the Muslim Turks. At first the Crusades were successful, establishing the Kingdom of Jerusalem. They were brutal and barbarian, however, and by their end in 1291 they had created a

---

2. To this day the Vatican, in the middle of the city of Rome, is given the status of an independent sovereign country, whose ruler is the pope. Most nations send an ambassador to the Vatican. This was a great thorn in the side of Mussolini and Hitler, because the Vatican remained neutral during World War II, and they did not dare invade it for fear of the wrath of the rest of the world.

hatred between Christians, Muslims, and Jews that plagues the world to this day. Before the Crusades there was relative peace and occasionally actual warmth between the three faiths.

The only positive aspect of the Crusades was that the Crusaders brought back from the East a wealth of learning and an appreciation of classical culture that had been lost during the Dark Ages in Europe. By the fourteenth and fifteenth centuries this had developed into a hunger for art and learning that overtook the whole of the Mediterranean world. We call this period the Renaissance, the "rebirth." It sparked a period of exploration and discovery that resulted in, among other things, the opening of Asia and the discovery of the Americas. It also threatened the power structure of the church as people discovered that "Holy Mother Church" did not have every answer to every question. As people began to question the teachings of the church, it undertook a "witch-hunt" for heretics called the Holy Inquisition, which in Spain reached a new low of human brutality.

As the challenge to the church's worldly authority grew, there also arose a challenge to her doctrines and practices. Men such as Wycliffe, Huss, Zwingli, Luther, and Calvin arose in an attempt to reform the church from within, but ultimately their movements resulted in schism and the formation of new branches of Christianity. Among the major groups that rose out of this were the Lutherans, Presbyterians, the Reformed churches, and Baptists. These retained the biblical basics of the faith, but repudiated much of the post-apostolic thinking and practice of the historic church. This was the start of the Protestant Reformation,[3] a movement that is generally considered to have begun officially in 1517 when Martin Luther nailed his Ninety-five Theses to the door of the church in Wittenberg, Germany.

Meanwhile, in Britain, the Protestant Reformation had considerably less influence than on the continent except for an incursion of Calvinist thinking in the north. In fact, Henry VIII wrote a brilliant refutation of Luther's teachings, and because of it the pope granted him the title "Defender of the Faith."[4] Henry subsequently had a major conflict

---

3. Luther was the first to use the term "Protestant." He called himself *Protestor Fidei*, a "Witness of the Faith." The term came into common use to refer to those who protested against the abuses of the Roman church.

4. As we will see in the chapter on Anglicanism, Henry VIII, for all his worldly

with the pope over the validity of his forced marriage to his brother's widow, Catherine of Aragon.[5] He ultimately resolved the conflict in 1534 by using some historic and theological loopholes to proclaim the archbishop of Canterbury, rather than the pope, the ultimate spiritual authority in England. He did not deny any of the other teachings or practices of the Roman Catholic Church, and to his death he considered himself a faithful Catholic. His actions were the beginning, however, of the Anglican Reformation, which ripened three monarchs later during the reign of Elizabeth I.

In 1545 the church struck back against the Protestant and Anglican Reformations, convening the Council of Trent in northern Italy. It supported a movement known as the Counter-Reformation, dedicated to dispelling heresy through doctrine and reason rather than by torture, the Inquisition's method. While much of the latter persisted, the Council of Trent, which met continuously for eighteen years, breathed a new life into theological thought in the Roman church. Although it produced some benighted ideas, it also produced some brilliant thinking that carried the church out of the Middle Ages and into the light of the Renaissance.

In much of Europe the Reformation made strong inroads, and many kings and rulers accepted Protestant ideas. The church, in grudging agreement with the Holy Roman Empire, finally acceded to the doctrine *cuius regio, eius religio* ("whose region, his religion"). This meant that the religion of the ruler automatically became the only legal religion of his realm. The idea of freedom of religion that we take so for granted was extremely rare, being found to any significant degree only in Holland and, later, in early colonial America in Pennsylvania and Maryland.[6] Though we take the concept of freedom of religion for

---

failings, was a superb theologian. His childhood dream was not to be king (he had an older brother who later died), but to be archbishop of Canterbury.

5. Henry VIII did not "found the Church of England in order to get a divorce." He had valid arguments for an annulment of his marriage to Catherine. The pope, for political reasons, would not consider them, so Archbishop Cranmer granted the annulment. The entity that we call the Church of England did not evolve until after Henry's death thirteen years later.

6. The claim that the Puritans and Pilgrims came to America for religious freedom is a myth. They came for their own religious freedom, but were completely intolerant of other religions. In the Pennsylvania charter, William Penn, a Quaker, in-

granted, it would not become commonplace until the late eighteenth century. Notwithstanding, the absolute hold of the Roman Catholic Church over western Europe was broken.

The period from the Reformation to the present, while it has generated a wealth of new ideas, points of view, and values, has also been an era of frequent schism. After the major breaks (such as that of the Lutherans and Calvinists from Rome, the Roman and Anglican separation, and the Methodists' break from the Church of England), the new movements themselves began to break apart. By the beginning of the twentieth century, for example, there were at least ten separate groups calling themselves Methodist and over fifteen Baptist groups. Many of the divisions in Protestantism occurred not only because of theological disputes, but also over issues of geography, politics, morals, and race.

It is encouraging to note that the latter half of the twentieth century was marked by strong ecumenical efforts. Two major mergers, in 1939 and 1968, reunited most of the disparate Methodist bodies into the United Methodist Church (UMC); in 1988 a series of previous mergers climaxed with the formation of the Evangelical Lutheran Church of America (ELCA), reuniting the majority of American Lutherans.

While the ecumenical movement began in earnest at the end of the nineteenth century, its first great surge forward began when Pope John XXIII convened the Second Vatican Council in 1962. This council dealt with questions of religious liberty, liturgical reform, and the role of the church in the modern world. It inspired most of Christianity with a desire to focus on areas of agreement rather than on differences. In response to a call from Pope John, several serious dialogues are now ongoing between a great variety of denominations, including the Roman Catholics and Anglicans. The recent agreement of intercommunion between the Episcopal Church and the ELCA also grew out of this dialogue. (This agreement is not a merger, but signifies active cooperation and a mutual recognition of the validity of

---

sisted on freedom for all religions, including Judaism. Maryland was formed as a refuge for persecuted Roman Catholics, but its charter also allowed the freedom to practice any religion. These were considered radical, if not dangerous, thoughts at the time.

each other's clergy and sacraments.) Similar dialogues and imminent intercommunions or mergers are in the offing for a number of Protestant groups.

The history of the church is a history of schisms. Perhaps now, by the grace of God, it can become one of growing unity. Our ultimate prayer is that of our Lord: that "they may be one even as we are one."

THE EASTERN ORTHODOX

The question of whether the oldest branch of Christianity is Roman Catholicism or Eastern Orthodoxy is moot. Both claim to be the oldest, and there are reasonable arguments on both sides. In fact, they both are continuous from the one apostolic church, becoming increasingly disparate through the first ten centuries. They were not recognized as separate branches of the faith until they excommunicated each other in 1054. The spiritual and administrative seat of the Roman Catholic Church is, of course, Rome. The spiritual seat of the Eastern churches is Constantinople,[1] but as in Anglicanism, there is an administrative seat for each of the autonomous national Orthodox bodies. The official name of the body is the Orthodox Catholic Church. One major difference between the Orthodox Church and Catholicism is that Roman Catholicism teaches that all spiritual authority comes from Christ through the pope, who is the Vicar of Christ and the ultimate authority in matters of faith and morals. Orthodoxy, on the other hand, considers the patriarch to be the first among equals, with no greater spiritual authority than any other

1. In 293 CE the Emperor Diocletian divided the Roman Empire. He selected Byzantium, an unimportant city in what is now Turkey, to be the seat of power in the eastern portion. In 313 the Emperor Constantine established his throne there, and in 330 renamed it Constantinople, although his realm was still called the Byzantine Empire. The city fell to the Turks in 1453, and in 1930 they renamed it Istanbul. Eastern Orthodoxy still refers to it ritually as Constantinople, and the archbishop is known as the patriarch of Constantinople.

bishop (similar to the role of the archbishop of Canterbury in Anglicanism).

By the end of the first millennium, Rome had degenerated to no more than a provincial town. Charlemagne had established the Carolingian Empire in 800, and in about a century that evolved into the Germanic "Holy Roman Empire." Rome had been shoved into the background, and the patronage of the old Roman Empire had long since degenerated into feudalism. This opened the way for the bishop of Rome, the pope, to take control of enormous power in the West. It offered, however, no competition to Constantinople as the true seat of Christian civilization from Naples north to the Danube and east through Palestine and Persia. Furthermore, the Byzantine church had extended its missions beyond the borders of the empire over the Caucasus and through Russia, all the way to the edge of the Asian continent.

In the course of these centuries differences in the customs and liturgies of the Roman and Byzantine churches had developed. The Western church was based solidly in ancient Roman thinking, while the Eastern church was thoroughly Hellenistic (Greek). A more important factor was that serious philosophical and theological differences had evolved, not the least of which was the role of the primary bishop (pope vs. patriarch). Byzantine power was growing rapidly in northern Italy and all around the Mediterranean. By the mid-eleventh century the patriarch of Constantinople, Michael Cerularius, was totally intolerant of the Latin church, suppressing it wherever he was able. His counterpart, Pope Leo IX, was equally close-minded. In 1054 an abortive attempt was made to reconcile the two churches. Differences of language, politics, culture, and practice proved to be too great, and the delegates finally ended by hurling anathemas (ecclesiastical curses) at each other. Leo excommunicated Cerularius and the entire Byzantine church.[2] Cerularius reciprocated by excommunicating the Roman church, thus confirming the Great Schism of 1054, the first major split in the Christian church.

Even then there was the possibility of reconciliation, but in 1099

---

2. In terms of relative size and power, this would be rather like the Episcopal Church excommunicating the archbishop of Canterbury and the entire worldwide Anglican Communion.

Latin Crusaders replaced the Orthodox prelates of Antioch and Jerusalem with Roman bishops; all hope of peace between the two was dashed in 1204 when Roman Crusaders, with Pope Innocent III's blessing, sacked Constantinople and enthroned a Venetian as patriarch. Attempts at reunion were made from time to time with little effect until 1452, when political pressure caused many Eastern patriarchs to submit to Roman authority, although most recanted soon thereafter.[3] In 1453 Constantinople fell to the Ottoman Turks, the cathedral was converted to a Muslim mosque, and there was little further communication with the Latin church thereafter. There appeared no hope of reconciliation whatsoever until 1965, when Pope Paul VI and Patriarch Athenagoras I both rescinded the excommunications of 1054; serious dialogues began between the two churches in 1968. Nevertheless, it will probably be a very long time before any real healing of the relationship can be expected.

Under the Ottomans, Christians were relatively well treated (unlike the westward sweep of Islam, under which Christians in many regions were forced to convert to Islam or die). Islam officially sees Christians and Jews as "people of the Book," recognizing their religions as valid but incomplete, although some Islamic groups consider Christians "infidels," worthy only of death. The Ottoman sultan permitted Orthodox worship under the ecclesiastical rule of the patriarchs.

There are few critical theological differences between Eastern Orthodoxy and western Catholicism. One major bone of contention in the sixth century was a dispute over whether the Holy Spirit proceeds[4] from the Father only (the Eastern view) or from the Father and the Son (the Western view). This dispute is at such a high theological level that it deals only with the subtlest of concepts. It centers around a phrase in the Nicene Creed known as the *"filioque* clause" (*filioque* is Latin for "and the Son"). Most theologians agree that the salvation of souls hardly depends on the resolution of this argument. In practice, however, it was and remains a symbol of the power struggle between East

3. The ones that remained loyal to Rome are called "Uniate" or "Eastern Rite" churches. Their allegiance is to the pope and to Roman Catholic theology, yet their liturgy and customs, including marriage of clergy, remain those of the Eastern tradition.

4. "Procession" is an arcane theological concept that refers to the original relationship of the Holy Spirit to the Father and the Son.

and West.[5] The phrase "and the Son" *(filioque)* was added to the Nicene Creed at the Council of Toledo (Spain) in 589. The addition was rejected by all the Byzantine delegates, but approved by all the Roman ones, who outnumbered the Byzantines; the Byzantine church refused to use the phrase. This event is generally regarded as the beginning of the events that climaxed in the Great Schism of 1054.

Eastern Orthodox and Catholic sacramental theology are essentially the same, although there are differences in emphasis and liturgical expression. The Eastern church places great emphasis on mystery, believing that religious truths cannot be fathomed by human reason, but only by divine revelation, and therefore must be accepted on faith. In contrast, the Western Church is very analytical, seeking to find an explanation of religious truths such as the presence of Christ in the Blessed Sacrament. Such explanations are often rooted in pre-Christian Greek philosophy. The effect of this difference is seen in the different liturgies (rituals and ceremonials) of the two. Eastern liturgy is steeped in mystic symbolism; for example, at the consecration of the Sacrament the priest goes behind an iconostasis, a beautifully decorated screen, where the sacrament is consecrated out of sight of the congregation to emphasize its mystery. There is also a difference in how Communion is administered. In the Orthodox church, a fragment of the Host is placed on a special spoon, the *labis*, dipped in the chalice, and fed to the communicant from the spoon. Eastern theology teaches that baptism and confirmation are inseparable, so an infant receives both sacraments at the same time. The Orthodox administer Communion to infants as soon as they are baptized and confirmed. (This practice is slowly making its way into Anglicanism, but is strongly resisted by many; one argument against it is that in the West children are not confirmed until they reach an "age of reason.")

Orthodoxy has the same structure of holy orders as does Roman Catholicism, that of bishops in the historic succession, priests, and deacons. Women are not accepted into holy orders. In most Orthodox bodies a married priesthood is allowed, but the marriage must take

5. In the 1970s the Episcopal Church proposed dropping the *filioque* clause from the Creed in the new revision of the Prayer Book, as a token of the warm relationship between Eastern Orthodoxy and Anglicanism. The resulting outcry indicated that this would be interpreted as an insult to Roman Catholicism, and the clause remained in the final version in 1979.

place before ordination. One may not marry after ordination, even if he is widowed, and no one who has been married more than once, for any reason including his wife's death, may be admitted to the priesthood. Bishops must be celibate, so married priests are automatically excluded from consideration for the episcopate.

Marriage is considered an eternal union, indissoluble even by death. It is celebrated with a rite of crowning at the altar, performed with great solemnity and beautiful ritual. Widowed people may remarry, but since the first spouse is considered the eternal one, second marriages are blessed with quite subdued and almost penitential ceremonies. Divorce is tolerated but discouraged, and only in the rarest of circumstances is remarriage permitted after divorce, even if the divorced spouse has died.

Another important difference between Eastern and Western practice is seen in the art forms of the two. In the West, any form of visual art is acceptable. In the East, however, art may only be two-dimensional. Statuary, reliefs, and engraving are not used. The result is that magnificent mosaic and painting styles have developed, usually in the form of "icons." Icons are stylized representations of people and events in Christian history and legendry.[6] In the eighth and ninth centuries a controversy arose in the Byzantine church, based on differing interpretations of the second commandment. The "Iconoclasts" ("destroyers of images") claimed that the use of images was idolatrous in that it automatically led to worship of those images. The opposite argument was that since Christ took on full visible humanity, divine manifestations can be described and venerated in art as well as in words. Known as the "Iconoclastic Controversy," the debate was finally ended in 843 when the widow of the Emperor Theophilus decreed that it was permissible to venerate two-dimensional images. The controversy did not reach the West to any significant degree, so statuary remained a common Western religious art form.[7] An important minor feast in the East is the

6. The formal definition of "icon," from the Greek *eikon,* "image," is "representation." The word has recently become best known as a computer term for a symbol representing a command.

7. During the Protestant Reformation this controversy did arise in the West, and many Protestant groups banned the use of any images; Cromwell destroyed religious art all over England. Today many Protestant churches are devoid of any graphic arts, including stained glass.

"Feast of Orthodoxy," celebrated on the first Sunday in Lent, commemorating the end of the Iconoclastic Controversy.[8]

The liturgical cycle of Orthodoxy, like that of the West, is centered around Easter, the feast of the resurrection, which is the seminal event of all Christianity. The date of Easter in the Orthodox tradition does not always coincide with that in the West. The date was fixed by the Council of Nicaea (325) as the first Sunday after the full moon following the spring equinox. The Eastern Orthodox liturgical calendar, however, is calculated by the Julian system rather than the Gregorian (which the West uses). This often causes a difference in dates. Also, Eastern tradition requires that Easter not precede or coincide with Passover. In the East, even more than in the West, every Sunday is celebrated as a "little Easter."

The Orthodox church pays significantly less attention to Christmas than does the Latin church, although there is much more festivity at Epiphany, January 6.[9] Epiphany is the commemoration of the visit of the magi, and it is at this time that people celebrate and exchange gifts. While Christmas as a secular feast has become extremely important in the West, it is only passingly observed in Eastern society.

Veneration of the Blessed Virgin is a central point of Orthodox spirituality, as it is in Roman Catholicism. Mary is referred to as *Theotokos*, "God Bearer," used in the same way as the Western *Mater Dei*, "Mother of God." This is not to imply (as some Protestants accuse) that she is believed to have begotten God or that she is deified. Rather, she is the mother chosen by God as the vessel to bear his Son, the woman through whom he imparted humanity to the divine Christ.[10]

Eastern Orthodoxy is steeped in tradition, causing some to accuse it of being out of touch with the modern world and its material and

---

8. In the Eastern church, art has a much greater spiritual significance than in the West. Icons are not simply painted or tessellated, they are "prayed." The artist undergoes a long spiritual preparation before making an icon and prays and studies Scripture diligently during its preparation. When the work is finished it is said that he has "prayed an icon."

9. Christmas was not even observed in the very early church, and did not become an important feast in the West until the early Middle Ages.

10. A similar idea is the modern expression "Mother of the Year." This does not mean that the mother being honored begot the year. Likewise, *Theotokos* or *Mater Dei* does not imply that Mary begot God.

spiritual needs. On the other hand, loyalty to the old ways of thinking and worshiping has given it the strength to bear up under countless threats. Because it has held fast to tradition, Eastern Orthodoxy has been a marvel of survival under centuries of invasion, oppression, and persecution. A classic example is the Russian Orthodox Church. It has endured Mongols, Tartars, Tsarist control, Bolsheviks, and the Soviet Union, and still thrives while these groups survive only in the pages of history.

THE ROMAN CATHOLICS

Much of what is taught and practiced in Roman Catholicism is also found in Eastern Orthodoxy and Anglicanism. I like to identify these three as the Catholic churches, as distinguished from the Protestant churches, which are for the most part descendants of the churches of the Protestant Reformation. Hereafter when we refer to "Catholic" we mean all three, as opposed to "Roman Catholic," which specifies the church in communion with the bishop of Rome, the pope.

Roman Catholicism, along with its sister Catholic branches, Orthodoxy and Anglicanism, can trace its origins back along an unbroken line directly to the first-century apostolic church. An overview of its early history can be found in the earlier "A Brief History of the Christian Church," so we will not repeat it here. The major turning points in Roman Catholic history were Arianism[1] (fourth century), the Great Schism[2] (eleventh century), the Reformation[3] (fifteenth–sixteenth centuries), and the developments during and after the Second Vatican Council[4] (mid–twentieth century).

1. At one time the majority of the church accepted the heresy of the Greek Arius (256?-336), which was quelled in the fourth century.

2. This was the schism that divided the church into Roman Catholicism and Eastern Orthodoxy.

3. The separation of the Anglican Church and the creation of Protestant denominations brought about an internal reformation as well.

4. There have been huge changes in liturgy and teaching since Vatican Council II (1962-65).

The belief system of all religions is based on faith, but this is a very difficult concept to define. Protestant bodies define faith as a confidence in the saving power of God's grace, a belief firmly rooted in the New Testament. Roman Catholicism, on the other hand, places its emphasis more in the teachings of Saint Augustine of Hippo. It teaches that faith is an intellectual assent to revealed truth (doctrine inspired by God in the minds of men). This teaching was firmly formulated by Saint Thomas Aquinas and ratified by the Council of Trent, and was an unshakable teaching until this century.[5] The Second Vatican Council (1962-65) shifted slightly from this position, adding to it the establishment of a personal relationship with God.

Theology draws a distinction between revelation as truth deduced from observation of nature and man (which is "philosophy"), and revelation as truth revealed directly to man by God through vision or divine inspiration. Roman Catholic theology places a much greater emphasis on the latter than do other Christian bodies. Most Protestant groups rely strictly on Scripture as the authority for the formation of doctrine. Anglicanism and Orthodoxy rely equally on Scripture, reason, and tradition, while Roman Catholicism relies also on divine revelation.[6]

In Roman Catholic theology, as in Orthodoxy, tradition is extremely important. The "deposit of faith" was made to the apostles, and direct revelation ceased with their death. There is no new revelation, but simply new understanding of that which has been already revealed.[7] Truth is interpreted and promulgated through the teaching authority of the church as protected by the pope and the college of bishops, inspired by the Holy Spirit. Tradition is the word of the church, and the Bible is the word of God. It is the responsibility of the church, guided by tradition, to interpret the Bible. (Ultimately, since

5. Anglicanism and Orthodoxy take a middle road between these two positions.

6. For a doctrine to be considered an essential belief in Protestantism it must be clearly *stated* in the Bible; in Anglicanism and in Orthodoxy, it must be traditional, reasonable, and clearly *supported* by the Bible; in Roman Catholicism, it must be traditional *or* stated in the Bible.

7. An analogy would be Newton's "discovery" of the law of gravity. He observed no more than what people had been observing for untold millennia, but he gave it a new interpretation that changed the whole face of science.

the church authenticated the Bible and not vice versa, the final authority lies in the church's interpretation of the Bible.) The Council of Trent (1545-63) affirmed that tradition and Scripture bear equal authority. This is in direct opposition to the Protestant doctrine of *sola Scriptura* ("the Bible alone"), which accepts only the Bible as a source of doctrine. Anglicanism and Orthodoxy accept both as equal but inseparable — a teaching must be traditional and clearly supported by the Bible in order to be considered essential.[8]

An important characteristic of the Roman Catholic Church is the *magisterium*, the teaching authority of the church, which rests in the pope and the bishops in communion with him. According to Roman Catholic theology, the *magisterium* is guided by the Holy Spirit to right teaching, and Roman Catholics therefore have a moral obligation to accept these teachings even if they do not always seem logical or reasonable to the individual believer. This concept is based on Jesus' teaching to the apostles, whom the church represents, when he said, "He who hears you hears me."

When most people consider the difference between Roman Catholicism and other Christian faiths, the first thing that usually comes to mind is the papacy. Whoever holds the seat of the bishop of Rome is called the pope, from the Italian *Papa*, "Father."[9] The pope is seen as the Vicar of Christ, meaning that he acts and speaks for Christ on earth. All ecclesiastical authority passes from Christ through him, then through the college of bishops, and finally to the lower orders. He is thus not only the chief bishop, but superior to all other bishops (unlike the archbishop of Canterbury and patriarch of Constantinople, who are leaders, but in every spiritual sense are deemed equal to all other

8. An example is the Roman Catholic dogma (required belief) of the Immaculate Conception, which states that Mary was conceived without the taint of original sin. This tradition goes back at least to the fourth century, but is only vaguely and indirectly implied in the Bible. Most Protestants reject it outright; Anglicans and Orthodox are free to believe it and celebrate it if they wish, but it is not considered a dogma or important belief because it is not scriptural. It was proclaimed dogma in the Roman Church by Pope Pius IX in 1854. Despite common misuse of the term, the doctrine of the Immaculate Conception is not a teaching about the conception of Jesus, which is called the Divine or Miraculous Conception.

9. *Padre* is the correct Italian term for "father." *Papa*, a familiar form, was used because Jesus referred to God with the familiar *Abba*, "Daddy" (Mark 14:36), not as *Ab*, "Father."

bishops). Papal authority and power have grown consistently over the centuries. By about the fifth century the bishop of Rome's power had increased so much that he felt he had the right to impose the traditions, liturgy, and will of the church in Rome on the bishops of all other regions. The ultimate papal power was achieved at the First Vatican Council in 1879, when it was declared that the pope, on those occasions when he chose to speak officially (*ex cathedra*, "from the chair"), could speak infallibly on matters of faith or morals. While this was more a political than a spiritual action, it secured huge power for the papacy. The method of selection of the pope is the same as that of medieval emperors. The College of Cardinals (like the medieval electors) elects a new pope after the death of the reigning one. He is usually chosen from their ranks, but does not have to be. The pope appoints the cardinals. A cardinal may be any baptized Christian, but is almost exclusively selected from among the bishops. In modern times no pope has been more loved by Protestants or Catholics than John XXIII, who precipitated the reform of the church in the 1960s; none has been more respected than the current pope, John Paul II.

As in the Orthodox and Anglican churches, there are three types of ordained clergy in the Roman Catholic Church — deacons, priests, and bishops — with the addition of the special role of the bishop of Rome. For the most part the clergy must be celibate, although there have been some very successful experimental programs with married deacons.[10] Some experimenting has been done (particularly in Holland) with married priests, but it is not likely that a married priesthood will be common in the near future. It is even more unlikely that women will be admitted to holy orders soon.

The doctrines of Roman Catholicism, like those of most other Christian faiths, are summed up in the Apostles' Creed. The body of teaching, of course, extends well beyond this summary. One important doctrine is that of original sin. Contrary to the common misunderstanding, this has nothing to do with the fact that humans reproduce sexually. It teaches that a basic trait of human nature (inherent from

10. Clerical celibacy was not always the practice of the church. It was recommended by the end of the second century, and required (but rarely enforced) by the fifth century. Only in the past four centuries has the rule been strictly enforced.

our origin) is the tendency to sin. As soon as we are capable of understanding that something can be objectively wrong, we will from time to time knowingly choose to commit such a wrong. Since it is inherent, it is in us from our conception. We can be delivered from it only by a saving act of God, and not through our own merits. Holy baptism is a gift of God, initiated by Jesus, that frees us of the responsibility for this spiritual flaw. Once baptized we are responsible only for the sins we commit, not for the flaw that leads us to commit sin. For this reason infants are baptized as soon as possible.[11]

One conflict between Roman Catholicism and much of the rest of Christianity deals with life after death, particularly with regard to Limbo and purgatory. In Roman Catholic theology, purgatory is the place where the faithful dead are sent to be cleansed from their sins and prepared for entrance into heaven. After those in purgatory have purged their sins through temporary punishment, they are received into heaven.[12] Limbo (though not an official Catholic doctrine) was traditionally thought of as a place in the afterlife in which good but unbaptized souls reside and in which there is neither punishment nor heavenly reward. Many believe that this is where innocents such as unbaptized babies go. Today the concept of Limbo is rejected by most Roman Catholic theologians. Purgatory, on the other hand, is widely accepted. Anglican and Orthodox theologians accept it with a slightly different interpretation — rather than a place of purgation, it is seen as a place of learning and spiritual growth in preparation for heaven. They usually refer to it as the "intermediate state" rather than as "purgatory." Most Protestants reject the concept totally, believing that there is no such "stepping-stone" between life on this earth and

11. Original sin is also an important doctrine in Eastern Orthodoxy, Anglicanism, and many Protestant denominations. Certain Protestant groups, rejecting the concept of original sin, see baptism more as an act of personal commitment to Christ than as a relief from a destructive flaw. For this reason, they object to infant baptism and baptize only when the person has reached an age at which he can make a voluntary commitment.

12. Virtually all "ordinary" Christians enter purgatory upon death. It is only those, such as saints, who have already succeeded in cleansing themselves from their sins in this life who enter heaven directly. It should also be noted that the "punishment" of purgatory is completely different from the punishment endured by the damned in hell.

heaven.[13] Thus, while many Catholics pray for the dead (to encourage them and give them strength to endure the trials of purgatory), Protestants typically remember but do not pray for the dead.

All of the Catholic churches rely heavily on the sacraments. These are outward signs that proclaim inner grace. Two, holy baptism and Holy Eucharist, are considered "major" or "greater" sacraments because they were specifically commanded by Jesus. The others, those sanctified by Jesus' actions or teaching but not commanded, are called "minor" or "lesser" sacraments. Of these there are generally considered to be five: holy confirmation, holy matrimony, holy orders (ordination), holy penance (confession), and holy unction (anointing of the sick). The number of sacraments had never been defined until the eleventh century, when seven was the number most commonly taught. When the Protestant reformers reduced it to only the two major sacraments, the Council of Trent officially defined it as seven, and that number is also accepted by the Orthodox, most Anglican, and some Lutheran churches. To this day most Protestants accept only two, baptism and Communion.

The central act of worship in the Roman Catholic Church has traditionally been the Holy Eucharist, commonly called the "Mass."[14] Many Protestant reformers replaced it with a prayer service based on ancient synagogue worship, but it has always been the main act of worship in Roman Catholicism and Orthodoxy; it has been restored as such in most of Anglicanism.[15] It is ironic that as instituted by Christ, the basis of the Eucharist is Christian unity symbolized by a community meal. Yet no Christian discipline, Catholic or Protestant, empha-

13. The doctrine of purgatory was not a major issue in the early days of the Reformation. Rather, the issue was its abuse by teaching that a person could reduce or eliminate his time in purgatory by good works or gifts of grace, known as "indulgences." The sale of indulgences as a fund-raising technique had reached a nadir of abuse by the time of the Reformation, and an attack on it was among Luther's Ninety-five Theses.

14. From the Latin *Missa*, derived from the word for "to send." "Eucharist" comes from the Greek *eucharistein*, "to give thanks."

15. For a long time the common Anglican worship was Morning Prayer, a service based on the monastic daily office of Matins. The early tradition of Anglicanism, however, was Mass, and this has now again become the primary form of Sunday worship.

sizes or even seriously encourages ecumenical unity in its Eucharistic ceremonial.

Until the twentieth century the language of the Mass was Latin. The first Eucharists had been in the universally understood language of the time, which was Greek. As the Eastern and Western churches became more and more at odds, the East retained the Greek and the West turned to the language of the Western empire, Latin, because regardless of their local tongue, everyone understood that language.[16] Long after it was no longer understood, it was retained for all official church business, including public worship. The Second Vatican Council set in motion the process that now requires the Mass to be celebrated in the local language of the people. In Eastern Europe there are several so-called "Uniate Churches," which are Eastern Orthodox churches in communion with the Roman Catholic Church (and thus out of communion with the rest of Eastern Orthodoxy). Although they accept Roman Catholic doctrine, these churches for centuries have been allowed to retain the full Eastern Orthodox practice and liturgy, including a married priesthood and the vernacular languages.

During the Middle Ages, because they did not understand Latin, the people became more and more observers of the Mass rather than participants in it. As a result, their understanding of it decreased, and thus the power of the clergy increased immensely. The least educated people looked on the Mass as an almost magical rite, to the extent that many of the Protestant reformers accused the clergy of practicing the black arts. This accusation is no longer taken seriously, of course, but it carried much power in its day.[17] People rarely received Holy Communion, so a rule was enacted that they must receive it at least once a year — this rule is still in effect today. This led to a custom that is now justly falling into disuse, the "non-communicating Mass," in which only the priest receives Communion. In order to prevent the blood of Christ from spilling and being desecrated, the people were not given the chalice when they received the Sacrament but received only the Host.

16. The Latin that was used was not the classical language (that of Virgil and Cicero), but a simple and somewhat corrupted version of late Latin known as Ecclesiastical or "Church" Latin.

17. At the consecration of the Host the priest repeats the words of Jesus, *"Hoc est enim corpus meum"* ("For this is my Body"). The word "hocus-pocus" is derived from this.

This practice was one major cause of criticism against the Roman Catholic Church at the time of the Anglican Reformation, but the chalice has slowly been restored to the people in more recent years.

Catholic theology (including Orthodox and Anglican) teaches the "Real Presence" — that the glorified (i.e., resurrected) Christ is objectively present in the Blessed Sacrament,[18] and thus it is treated with the utmost reverence, as are all the vessels and linens used in conjunction with it. In the Roman Catholic Church the official explanation of how Christ is present is called transubstantiation. This is simply an explanation of *how*, not a statement *that*, he is present.[19] Anglicans and Orthodox do not attempt to define how, but simply accept the mystery of his presence. Most Protestants (except the Lutherans) teach that his presence is subjective — in other words, it depends on the faith of the believer. In all Roman Catholic and Orthodox, most Anglican, and some Lutheran churches the Sacrament is "reserved" (kept in a sacred chest on or near the altar) rather than being completely consumed at the end of the Mass. This is not only for convenience in case of emergency (sickness or accident), but as a reminder that Christ is perpetually with us. It also serves as a focus for prayer and meditation.

Veneration of the saints is a central practice of Roman Catholicism, as it is of Anglicanism and Orthodoxy. Basic to all these faiths is a belief in the "communion of the saints."[20] While some superstitious peo-

---

18. This means that Christ's presence does not depend on the faith of the receiver (although the benefit gained by receiving it does). He is fully present in his resurrected body and blood.

19. The doctrine of transubstantiation is based on Aristotelian philosophy via St. Thomas Aquinas. It teaches that while the outward and visible appearance ("accidents") of the bread and wine remain unchanged, the inner and invisible spiritual properties ("substance") become changed to those of the glorified Body and Blood of Christ. Early Lutherans and Calvinists dabbled with the concept of consubstantiation, that the substance of bread and wine remain, but that the consecrated Sacrament also bears the substance of the Body and Blood (Lutheran and Reformed theologians generally reject this today). Henry VIII argued that this is philosophically untenable, and that it is not given to man to understand or presume to explain how Christ is present — most Anglican theologians agree.

20. This is a tenet of the Apostles' Creed, to which most Protestants subscribe. Nevertheless, many Protestants are very uncomfortable with the concept, interpreting the phrase in the Creed as meaning only the community of the living faithful.

ple may abuse the practice, it should not in any way be confused with worship of the saints, which would be a violation of the first commandment. Holding the saints up as examples of godly life is in no way offensive to Protestantism. Asking their intercession would be, however, since most Protestants would consider the practice an adulteration of Christ as mediator. That is actually an oversimplification of the doctrine, however. The doctrine of the communion of the saints teaches that just as we who still live are one in Christ ("We are one body in Christ, Rom. 12:5), so we are one with those who have gone before. If it is acceptable to ask someone in this life to pray for us, then there should be nothing wrong with asking it of someone in the next life.

Veneration of the Virgin Mary plays a key role in Roman Catholic spirituality, at least as much as in Eastern Orthodoxy. She is referred to as *Mater Dei* ("Mother of God"), and her perpetual undefiled virginity is fiercely defended.[21] Roman Catholicism has been unjustly accused of "Mariolatry," worship of Mary. While some superstitious Roman Catholics may practice this, it is soundly condemned by the church — only God may be worshiped. Veneration of Mary honors her as queen of the saints, but does not condone treating her as a deity.

In 1962 Pope John XXIII convened the Second Vatican Council, which was an important event in "modernizing" the Roman Catholic Church. Among many significant actions, one of the most prominent was the new emphasis on ecumenism. The council instituted dialogues with Protestants, Anglicans, and Orthodox, and these groups in turn began dialogues with each other.[22] There has also been a widespread liturgical reform, restoring many liturgical rites and ceremonies to forms much more reflective of the original ancient ones. Experimentation in this area has led to some unsatisfactory results, but great progress has nevertheless been made. There has been conflict over many of the decisions of the council, including tension between those

21. Most Protestants defend the teaching that Mary was a virgin when Jesus was conceived, but believe that she established a normal marital relationship with Joseph after Jesus' birth. Some Protestants challenge even the virgin birth of Jesus. On the other hand, some defend Mary's perpetual virginity.

22. One recent result of this was the agreement of intercommunion between the Episcopal Church and the Evangelical Lutheran Church of America.

who want to modernize the liturgy and those who want to restore the traditional Latin Mass.

The post-council era has had other serious problems, not the least of which is an increasing conflict between the lower and hierarchical clergy, and between the clergy and laity, especially with regard to the issue of obedience. The lower clergy and the laity now demand more voice in critical ecclesiastical decisions. The old days when no priest would question a bishop and no layman would question a priest are gone, probably forever. There is also agitation among the clergy to abolish the celibacy rule. The positive side of these conflicts is a growing awareness of individual responsibility rather than a simple obedience to rules from above.

It has been said that the greatest mistake the Roman Catholic Church has made is that it treats all its members like children, while the greatest mistake of Protestantism is that it treats them like adults. The Second Vatican Council took great steps toward remedying that situation. Still, Protestants and Anglicans, who belong to churches that developed during the Renaissance, a time of new emphasis on learning and on the individual, sometimes have trouble comprehending the Roman Catholic Church's understanding of authority and hierarchy. Nevertheless, that church's stability, its contribution to human spirituality, and indeed its very survival are manifest marks of the hand of God.

THE LUTHERANS

Lutheranism can be said to espouse the purest form of Protestantism, the term "Protestant" having been coined by Martin Luther. He called himself *Protestor Fidei*, "A Witness to the Faith." Ironically, Lutheranism is more closely wedded to traditional Catholicism than any of the other Protestant denominations. But for its having turned away from an episcopate in the apostolic succession, it would be reasonable to identify it as one of the Catholic churches, along with the Eastern Orthodox, Roman Catholic, and Anglican Churches. The term "Lutheran" was originally used as a pejorative by the enemies of the movement.[1] Luther hated it, calling his movement the Evangelical Church of the Augsburg Confession. Eventually his followers adopted the name Lutheran, however, and treated it as an honored term.

Martin Luther

Martin Luther (1483-1546) is generally identified as the father of Protestantism. While he was not the first to confront the authority of the Roman Catholic Church, it was he who crystallized the growing unrest and began what came to be known as the Protestant Reformation. He was born and educated in Eisleben, Germany, and completed his master's studies and entered law school in 1505. Soon thereafter he had a

---

1. "Christian" and "Methodist" were also originally pejoratives.

life-changing religious experience, left his law studies, and entered the Augustinian monastery at Erfurt. He was ordained a priest in 1507 and was assigned to teach theology at the University of Wittenberg in Saxony. On a trip to Rome he was appalled by the spiritual laxity and abuses of ecclesiastical power he found there. One that particularly disturbed him was the sale of indulgences to raise funds for the building of St. Peter's Basilica in Rome. An indulgence was originally the remission of worldly punishment for sins that had been absolved. This idea was corrupted in the Middle Ages with the idea that the church could remit spiritual punishment as well. It was further corrupted when greedy ecclesiastics discovered that the cash sale of indulgences could be an endless source of revenue. Luther returned to Wittenberg in great fear for his salvation. He even resorted to whipping himself to purge himself of sin,[2] and he intensified his study and meditation on the Bible. He eventually realized that salvation is purely a gift of God, and that it depends upon faith, not human works. No good works or self-punishment could be sufficient to earn salvation, which is given freely to those whose faith leads them to seek it. This put him in direct conflict with the sellers of indulgences.

In 1517 Johann Tetzel arrived in Saxony to promote a campaign to sell indulgences for the building of Saint Peter's. He established a virtual marketplace for salvation in the town square of Wittenberg. This so revolted Luther that on October 31 he nailed to the door of the university chapel a challenge to the church, particularly to Tetzel, to debate what Luther saw to be ninety-five abuses of theology, Scripture, and ecclesiastical authority. The document came to be known as the Ninety-five Theses. While many agreed with him, including leading thinkers at Wittenberg and other German universities, the church ignored him. His protests became broader, however, and several attempts were made to come to a reconciliation as he increasingly demanded reform in the church. As Europe was moving out of the Middle Ages into the Renaissance, nationalism was growing. Luther demanded a release of papal control, asserting that the German church should be controlled by Ger-

2. Called "autoflagellation," this was a common practice during the Middle Ages. Believing that the black plague was God's punishment for man's sinfulness, flagellation societies arose in about 1250 in which penitents would walk from town to town chanting, carrying huge crosses, and whipping themselves raw. This continued for over three centuries.

mans. On October 6, 1520, he laid the final straw on the back of the Roman camel when he published *Prelude on the Babylonian Captivity of the Church*, in which he attacked the entire authoritative and sacramental structure of the Roman Catholic Church. In 1521 he was summoned before the Diet of Worms, where he made his classic statement, "Here I stand. I can do no other." A bull of condemnation, *Exsurge Domine*, was drawn up, and he publicly burned it in the Wittenberg city square. He was summarily excommunicated, and a warrant for his arrest was published. He took refuge in Wartburg Castle under the protection of the Elector Friedrich III of Saxony. During this time he translated the New Testament and part of the Old into German.

As the word spread, Luther found more and more supporters. Support for him grew so strong that the church did not dare prosecute him for fear of a widespread popular rebellion. The warrant was lifted, and Luther returned to Wittenberg, where he remained for most of the rest of his life. In 1526 he married Katharina von Bora, a former nun. They raised six children.

During his remaining years, Luther wrote extensively, including letters, theological expositions, liturgies, sermons, hymns, and two catechisms. He was intransigent about any theological point, however. Because of the lack of dialogue with those who disagreed with him — the fault of both sides — the Reformation that he launched eventually went off in several directions. This produced a number of Reformation movements, including the Calvinists, Anabaptists, and Anglicans. While they had many beliefs in common, each began to develop its own theology and traditions.

In his later years, plagued by ill health and painful stomachaches, Luther turned more and more of the leadership over to his disciple Philipp Melanchthon. At the Diet of Augsburg in 1530, Melanchthon, with Luther's blessing, produced the Augsburg Confession. This is a statement of the faith of the church that is still a guideline today for most Lutherans and is the normative expression of biblical doctrine for the Lutheran Church Missouri Synod and Wisconsin Evangelical Lutheran Synod. Luther was the moral and spiritual inspiration of the movement he launched, but he took little actual leadership of it during his last years, and it was Melanchthon who handled most of the administrative duties. Luther died in Eisleben, the town in which he had been born, in 1546.

Luther's legacy was not only that he managed to break the seemingly unshakable power of the papacy, but also that his social and theological concepts laid the groundwork for a new German society, and that his writings became established as a standard that would be a major influence on the modern German language.

History

Charles V, the Holy Roman Emperor,[3] was too busy defending his Habsburg empire from Turkish attack to devote himself to the suppression of Lutheranism. As a result, despite condemnation by the Edict of Worms in 1521, the movement grew rapidly throughout Europe. Many European princes embraced the new thinking. In 1555 the Peace of Augsburg was signed, by which the Holy Roman Empire agreed to the doctrine of *cuius regio, eius religio* ("whose region, his religion"). This meant that the religion of a given realm would be that of its local prince. (Religious freedom was at that time an unheard-of concept.) This allowed much of the leadership of the Lutheran movement to fall into the hands of the princes. It relieved the pressure of persecution and inquisition that had plagued Europe, but it caused considerable confusion as thrones and duchies shifted back and forth between Roman Catholic and Protestant rulers.

The Peace of Augsburg quieted things for the moment, but religious tensions still festered for another half-century. They finally erupted in 1618 in the Thirty Years' War, perhaps the most destructive conflict in European history. In 1648 the Peace of Westphalia finally ended the war. Lutheranism survived, primarily as a result of the intervention of Lutheran King Gustav II Adolph of Sweden and, ironically, that of Roman Catholic France, which sided with the Protestants for political reasons.

During the next centuries Lutheran thinking was shaped by many great theologians, primary among whom were Friedrich Schleier-

3. As a point of interest, Charles V was the grandson of Ferdinand and Isabella of Spain, nephew of Catherine of Aragon, and first cousin of Mary Tudor ("Bloody Mary") of England. He obtained the throne of the Holy Roman Empire by bribing the electors.

macher (1768-1834), Paul Tillich (1886-1965), Karl Barth (1886-1968), Martin Niemöller (1892-1984), and Dietrich Bonhoeffer (1906-45), who was martyred by the Nazis. It also had a significant influence on music, producing such men as Bach, Buxtehude, and Praetorius, and on philosophy, being represented by Kant, Hegel, Kierkegaard, and many others.

The first Lutherans to arrive in America came to New Amsterdam with the Calvinist Dutch settlers, who were reasonably tolerant of the Lutherans. The next wave was a group of settlers in Delaware, but the first major influx of Lutherans was at the beginning of the eighteenth century, when large numbers of German Lutherans immigrated to Pennsylvania. In 1748 they set up the first American synod. During the next 150 years Lutherans of all national backgrounds flooded into America, bringing their own customs and languages, and forming their own ethnic synods. By the beginning of the twentieth century there were disparate synods representing all the Scandinavian, Teutonic, and Slavic nations. A unification movement began after World War I, rapidly gaining momentum after World War II. Mergers took place throughout this period, especially in the 1980s. By 1988 there were still several small groups, but only three major groups: the Evangelical Lutheran Church of America (ELCA), the Lutheran Church Missouri Synod (LCMS), and the Wisconsin Evangelical Lutheran Synod (WELS).[4] The ELCA is the largest group, with over 5 million members. The LCMS has about 2.5 million, and the WELS about half a million, making Lutheranism the third largest Protestant denomination in America.[5] The Baptists are the largest with over 38 million members, and the Methodists second with 13.5 million.

---

4. The LCMS and WELS strictly interpret the Bible, Luther's teachings, and the *Book of Concord*. They were formed by German immigrants in Missouri and Wisconsin in the mid-nineteenth century in response to the incursion of rationalism into mainstream Lutheranism. They worked closely together until 1961, when disagreements led them to separate.

5. The world picture is somewhat different. According to the 1994 World Christian Encyclopedia, about a third of the world's population is Christian. Of these the largest group is Roman Catholic (54%), then Eastern Orthodox (10%), third is Lutheranism (3%), and fourth is Anglicanism (2.8%).

Customs and Beliefs

Lutheranism is a "confessional church," meaning that its statement of faith is written and specifically defined. This is found in a collection of nine documents: the Apostles', Nicene, and Athanasian Creeds; the unaltered Augsburg Confession (1530); the Apology of the Augsburg Confession (1531); Luther's Large Catechism (1529); Luther's Small Catechism, intended for children (1529); the Articles of Smalkald (1537); and the Form of Concord (1577). This collection was first published as *The Book of Concord* in 1580 by order of the Elector Augustus of Saxony.

A primary belief of Lutherans is shared with other Protestant groups. This is *sola Scriptura*, "Only the Bible," which states that doctrine must be based solely on the Bible and not on any other source (such as tradition or nonbiblical revelation).[6] Lutherans do, however, place great value on tradition, human reason, and the revelation of the Holy Spirit as God-given tools for the interpretation and understanding of Scripture. Along with the rest of Protestantism, they also accept the doctrines, emphasized by Luther, of *sola gratia* ("grace alone") and *sola fides* ("faith alone"). These deny that salvation or justification can be obtained by anything other than God's free gift of grace. In other words, there is no justification by good works — good works are evidence of faith, but have no value by themselves. This was a critical belief to Luther and his disciples. They accused the Roman church of teaching salvation by good works, and the Reformed (Calvinist) churches of teaching salvation by moral purity, which is also a form of good works. To Luther the relationship between God and the redeemed is wholly at God's initiative and through his grace, and man has no part in it but to accept it gratefully and to respond to it with righteousness.[7]

---

6. Roman Catholicism accepts the Bible, tradition, and revelation as equal doctrinal sources.

7. Luther believed adamantly in justification by faith alone, and was troubled by James 2:14-26, which seems to support justification by good works. In his first translation of the New Testament he did not translate this passage, which his detractors called "editing with a penknife." He resolved the problem by interpreting the verse to mean that good works are the truest evidence of an already existing faith.

Lutherans generally accept only the two sacraments mandated by Christ, baptism and Communion. They do have rites of marriage, ordination, confirmation, confession, and penance, recognizing a distinctly sacred overtone to them. These are not seen as essential activities for a balanced Christian spiritual life, however. Infant baptism is the norm, in recognition that salvation is a free gift of God, totally independent of the physical, moral, or intellectual accomplishments of the individual. The Lutheran church recognizes baptisms administered by any Christian denomination, as long as water was used, the Trinity was invoked, and the intention was to baptize as Christ commanded.

Unlike most other Protestant bodies, Lutherans believe in the doctrine of the Real Presence — the real and objective presence of the risen and ascended Christ "in, with, and under" the elements of bread and wine in the Holy Eucharist. While the spiritual benefit of receiving Communion is dependent upon the faith of the recipient, the presence of Christ is not. This is a belief which Lutherans share with all the Catholic churches, but which is rejected by the majority of other Protestants. The Roman Catholic explanation of the real presence is called transubstantiation and is based upon a medieval interpretation of Aristotelian philosophy. It teaches that at the consecration of the Sacrament a mystic and indescribable essence of the bread and wine, called the "substance," is replaced by the substance of Christ's Body and Blood. Luther taught that the substance of the bread and wine remain unchanged, but that at the consecration Christ's Body and Blood become co-present with the bread and wine.[8] Luther's disciple Philipp Melanchthon later used the ancient term "consubstantiation" to refer to this.[9] Lutherans today reject the

8. This was first proposed by Berengarius in the eleventh century. Luther suggested the concept in *The Babylonian Captivity of the Church*, and it was one of Henry VIII's objections to Luther's teachings. Henry's reply, *An Assertion of the Seven Sacraments*, caused Pope Clement II to award him the title, "Defender of the Faith." This, of course, preceded Henry's rebellion against papal authority.

9. Luther may well not have intended to imply a concept of consubstantiation in his writings, and Melanchthon did not use the term in the strict theological sense. In the *Articles of Smalkald,* Luther wrote, "As regards transubstantiation, we care nothing about the sophistical subtlety by which they teach that bread and wine leave or lose their own natural substance. . . . For it is in perfect agreement with Holy Scriptures that there is, and remains, bread" (Article VI, trans. Robert E. Smith).

use of the term "consubstantiation," and they accept Christ's presence without formal theological explanation, as the Anglicans and Orthodox do.

Lutheran worship is defined as "the assembly of believers among which the Gospel is preached and the Holy Sacraments are administered according to the Gospel" (Augsburg Confession, VII). The traditional liturgy is similar to the Roman Catholic Mass (and to the Episcopal Rite II). At first Luther wanted to retain the use of Latin in public worship, but he soon recognized the value of using the vernacular and wrote his liturgies in German. As a result, preaching on the scriptural lessons (which the people could now understand) took on a much stronger role than was found in Roman Catholicism at the time. It is still a valued part of Lutheran worship.

Lutheranism places great value on education, and since its early days has sponsored not only extensive Christian education programs for its members, but also schools and universities around the world. It is also deeply involved in missions and in social and relief work on a worldwide basis.[10]

Luther taught the doctrine of the "priesthood of all believers," that all Christians, male and female, by virtue of their baptism, are priests of God, and exercise that priesthood through their various vocations and roles in life by living and ministering as Christ taught us. The role of *pastor* (Latin for "shepherd") is not sacramental, but is contingent upon a call from God and the recognition of the congregation of the faithful. Lutheran clergy may marry. Church organizations vary from country to country and synod to synod. Some are congregational, some presbyterian, and some episcopal. The title of bishop does not imply a threefold ministry[11] or a bishop in the historic succession, but is more an administrative title. This is an area that is being deeply reexamined and redefined in the current dialogues between the ELCA and the Episcopal Church. Most Lutherans see the threefold ministry

10. The Episcopal Diocese of Alabama and the local ELCA have established a disaster response program, pooling their resources and working in full cooperation with each other. Similar cooperative programs exist all over the country.

11. The term "threefold ministry" refers to a sacramentally ordained clergy that consists of three different orders — bishops in the historic succession, priests, and deacons.

as an acceptable concept but of little importance, while Anglicans regard it as essential.[12]

Lutheranism, like Anglicanism, has sought the best of both Catholicism and Protestantism in trying to discern the truth into which the Holy Spirit promised to lead us. They are in many respects sisters in the faith, and they seek to continue to strengthen that bond.

---

12. The ELCA and the Episcopal Church have recently entered into full communion with one another. This is not the same as merging, but means that each will recognize the validity of the other's sacraments and clergy. The Episcopal Church has been in full intercommunion with the Swedish Lutheran Church for years.

THE ANGLICANS

Anglicanism can be considered the third, most recently developed, and smallest branch of the "Catholic church," the other two branches being Eastern Orthodoxy and Roman Catholicism. Like them, the Anglican church can trace its unbroken episcopate and traditional catholic faith directly back to the first-century apostolic church.

The Great Schism, the division between the Orthodox and Roman Catholic churches, was not a single event, but the result of a series of events from the fourth through the thirteenth centuries. It is difficult to assign a single date to it, but if we had to do so, it would be 1054, the year each of these bodies excommunicated the other. The parting of the ways between Anglicanism and Roman Catholicism, likewise, was the result of events ranging from the sixth through the seventeenth centuries. If a single event had to be named to identify the split, however, it would be Henry VIII's denial of papal authority in England in 1532.

The first authentic records of Christian churches in England date back to the early third century, although there is evidence that the church had established itself there by at least the middle of the second. By the sixth century a Celtic liturgy and tradition was widespread throughout the British Isles, and a strong influence from Eastern Orthodoxy was felt, particularly in the monasteries. In order to affirm the power of the papacy over that of Constantinople, in 597 Pope Gregory the Great sent Augustine, who would become the first archbishop of Canterbury, to bring the British into the Roman

102

fold.[1] The next ten centuries saw repeated power struggles between the papacy and the English throne. While most of the continental states readily swore fealty to the pope, England refused to do so until Pope Innocent III placed England under interdict in 1208. This meant that no ecclesiastical services, including burials, were allowed. Anyone violating the interdict was automatically excommunicated and deemed eternally damned. The interdict lasted for five years, while the decomposing bodies were literally stacked up outside the cemeteries. In 1213 King John Plantagenet[2] yielded, submitting England to papal vassalage. For the next three centuries English kings would wrestle with papal power, but with no success until the time of Henry VIII. He would use John's submission as an argument against papal rights in England, claiming that since the fealty was obtained under duress (the interdict) it was invalid.

All the movements to reform the church were rooted in the writings of the fourteenth-century radical English theologian John Wycliffe and those of his contemporary, the Czech Jan Hus. Both men condemned the abuses of the church, believed in predestination, and proclaimed the Bible as the sole source of doctrine. The Protestant Reformation that had begun to seethe on the continent by the sixteenth century offended Henry VIII, who wrote many works in opposition to it. It had a strong influence in Scotland, but was only weakly received in England, which remained faithful to the Roman Catholic Church.

The Origins of the Church of England

Although Henry VIII's motivation in breaking with the Church of Rome was surely in part because of his desire to obtain a divorce, he

---

1. This Augustine was not the same man as Augustine of Hippo, church father and author of *The City of God*.

2. This was the same John of Robin Hood fame, the younger brother of King Richard I, "the Lionheart." While far from being a great king, he was not as evil as legend has portrayed him. The interdict severely damaged his reputation. People blamed him for the sufferings that were actually caused by Rome's effort to force England into submission. Two years later, in 1215, he was forced by the barons to sign the Magna Carta. This might well not have happened if the barons had not been encouraged by the people's anger at John.

did have a theological basis for doing so. Because this latter fact is so often ignored, I will attempt to dispel some of the mythology surrounding the event by going into some detail about Henry's role in the Anglican Reformation.

Henry was the younger son of Henry VII Tudor, whose victory in the Wars of the Roses in 1485 had unified England after half a century of strife and civil war. The elder Henry was a lesser nobleman of the House of Lancaster and was strongly supported by the growing middle class. After defeating Richard III Plantagenet he married Elizabeth, a princess of the House of York, thus uniting the two warring families. She bore him two sons. The elder, Arthur, was heir to the throne, and the younger, Henry, was to be groomed to become archbishop of Canterbury. Even as a young boy Henry was fascinated with ecclesiastical and theological issues, and he dreamed of becoming archbishop.

In November of 1501, Arthur married the daughter of Ferdinand and Isabella of Spain, Catherine of Aragon, thus assuring peace between the old enemies England and Spain. Three months later, however, Arthur died, and eleven-year-old Henry became heir to a throne he did not want. The following year Pope Julius II granted a papal dispensation for Prince Henry to marry Catherine. It was against church law for a man to marry his brother's widow, but Rome could not afford a war between England and Spain, so the dispensation was granted on the probably false grounds that the marriage with Arthur had never been consummated.[3] Neither Henry nor his father was happy about this arrangement, although Henry VII strongly urged the union because the Spanish alliance was necessary for England's prosperity, if not her survival.[4] The marriage did not take place until after Henry VII's death.

A few weeks after Henry VIII ascended the throne in 1509, he married Catherine, who was seven years his senior. He worried about what he considered a violation of God's law, but since he had a papal dispensation and a friendly relationship with her he went ahead with

3. Privacy was not a privilege of princes in those days. The evidence of the consummation of a royal marriage (including stained sheets) was witnessed to assure its validity. The affidavits of the consummation of Arthur's and Catherine's marriage mysteriously disappeared shortly after Arthur's death.

4. At one point Henry VII even contemplated marrying Catherine himself in order to preserve peace between England and Spain.

the marriage. She produced several children, but all save one, Mary (1516), were stillborn or died at birth. Henry took this and the fact that there was no male heir as signs that the marriage was cursed. By this time he had become obsessed with producing a male heir. Also, he had an eye for young women (and had kept a number of mistresses), and although there is evidence that he bore no antipathy toward Catherine, he had long since lost any of the affection for her that he might have had in earlier years. In 1527, having become bored with the aging Catherine, and realizing that he, too, was beginning to age, he sought an annulment of the marriage. This is quite different from a divorce. A divorce dissolves a marriage, while an annulment is a statement that a true marriage had never existed in the first place. The archbishop of Canterbury had the authority to grant annulments, but Henry chose to turn to Rome in order to placate Spain and avoid any international repercussions.

This decision would change world history. The Holy Roman Emperor Charles V, Catherine's nephew, opposed the annulment on the grounds that it was an insult to Spain. He had defeated Pope Clement VII, who was being held under house arrest and did not dare offend his captor. The pope refused the annulment, claiming that the original dispensation was valid. Upon an appeal in 1528 the Lord Chancellor of England, Cardinal Thomas Wolsey,[5] was appointed to try the case in London. The case finally went to Rome in 1529, and it became apparent that the annulment would again be refused. During this time Henry's eye had fallen on the queen's young and beautiful lady-in-waiting, Anne Boleyn. Henry decided to turn to the archbishop of Canterbury for the annulment, but Wolsey, recognizing that it was too late, opposed this move. Henry discharged him and appointed his friend Sir Thomas More as chancellor, confident that More would support him. More refused to make any statement for or against the annulment. When pressed to do so he resigned as chancellor and retired to private life. He had such a reputation for integrity that his endorsement would have engendered huge support for the

---

5. Wolsey was hedonistic, ambitious, and a consummate politician. He attempted to keep Henry's regard and curry favor with the pope and the emperor at the same time. His failure cost him his influence with Henry. He eventually was accused of treason, but he died before being sent to the Tower.

annulment among Parliament and the people, who loved Catherine. More's silence so angered Henry that he tried to force his hand by having him imprisoned and tried. The perfidy of the king's secretary, Thomas Cromwell,[6] however, and the perjury of a petty bureaucrat, Richard Rich, brought about More's conviction and execution for treason in 1535.[7] Meanwhile, a respected Cambridge scholar priest, Thomas Cranmer, supported Henry and sought support for him from the European universities.

In 1532 Henry formally repudiated papal authority in England, declaring himself the head of the church *in* (not *of*) England, based on the fact that English fealty to the pope had been signed by John under duress in 1213, and was thus invalid. He argued that throughout history it was apparent that England had been independent of Rome, and he was simply officially recognizing that independence. He forced the clergy to acknowledge his supremacy and appointed Cranmer archbishop of Canterbury. Cranmer averred that the king was supreme in all matters of the church in England. Cranmer granted the annulment in 1533, five months after Henry had secretly married Anne Boleyn. The pope drew up a bull of excommunication of Henry, but it was never issued. Henry forced Parliament to enact the Acts of Succession, declaring Anne to be the queen and their offspring to be heirs to the throne. He dissolved the powerful monasteries, which had been loyal to the pope. He seized their property (a vast fortune), distributing much of it to the nobles who had supported him.

When he broke with the pope, Henry carried most of the English church with him. The most notable exceptions were St. Thomas More and St. John Fisher, the bishop of Rochester, who also refused to acquiesce and was executed for treason in 1535. A few monks and priests were put to death, but for the most part the clergy and laity were happy to be free from the papacy without having to submit to Protestant teachings.

It is important to note that to the day he died Henry considered

6. Cromwell became a patron of a poor Welsh family named Williams, and through his help they rose to wealth and power. In gratitude they took the name Cromwell. Their great-great-grand-nephew, Oliver Cromwell, led the revolution that murdered King Charles I in 1649. Oliver and his son Richard were dictators of England until the Restoration in 1660.

7. More was canonized a saint by the Roman Catholic Church in 1935.

himself a Catholic. His argument was not with the faith, but with papal power. He was ill-tempered and licentious, and a tyrant in both public and private life. He was nevertheless a fine scholar and musician, and a learned theologian.[8] He strongly resisted the Protestant Reformation both in England and abroad. He was a brilliant politician, albeit ruthless in the way that he played factions against one another.

Cranmer had been influenced by much of the continental Protestant thinking, and he wanted to reform the church, but Henry kept him well under control. Henry encouraged the correction of abuses (such as the sale of indulgences and the raging nepotism among the higher clergy), but he was very defensive of traditional Catholic theology and would allow no change in practices or teachings that had a sound theological basis. He supported the dismantling of the monastic orders on the basis that they had been the source of much of the corruption in the church. They also controlled vast wealth that Henry wanted. Another major change he supported was the translation of the Bible and all services into English. Had he lived longer the first Book of Common Prayer might have been produced under his authority, but this would not come about until two years after his death.[9]

The only child that Anne Boleyn bore Henry was Elizabeth, who would eventually rank among England's greatest rulers. Henry tired of Anne when after three years there was no son. He was now forty-five (getting old, by the standards of that era) and he was impatient for a son. He was convinced that a woman could not rule England well. In 1536, the year that Catherine of Aragon died, he tacitly permitted a conspiracy to have Anne convicted of adultery and executed for treason (charges of which historians agree she was innocent). Two weeks after the execution he married another lady-in-waiting, Jane Seymour. The following year she bore him a son, Edward, but she died a few

---

8. To this day the English sovereign bears the title "Defender of the Faith." This was bestowed on Henry and all his successors by Pope Clement II (before the annulment) in honor of a brilliant theological treatise, *Assertion of the Seven Sacraments,* that Henry wrote in refutation of Martin Luther's *Babylonian Captivity of the Church.*

9. Archbishop Cranmer, virtually by himself, translated and compiled the first Prayer Book. It was his greatest achievement. Not only is it a brilliant piece of liturgical scholarship, but it is deemed one of the greatest literary works ever produced in the English language.

days later from complications of childbirth. It is said that she was not very bright but was very gentle and sweet. She was probably the only woman that Henry ever truly loved, and he was devastated by her death.[10] Edward, being a male, automatically became Henry's heir over Mary and Elizabeth; his reign, while short, would be a significant milestone in the history of the Church of England.

Henry died in 1547. Despite his personal life, his official acts left the church in England truly Catholic, yet truly reformed. He was succeeded by his nine-year-old son, Edward VI. Since Edward was too young to rule, Parliament appointed a regent, the Duke of Somerset, and later the Duke of Northumberland. Both men were unscrupulously power-hungry and greedy. They saw in Protestantism an opportunity to plunder the church and keep it under their control. They gave Cranmer the chance he had been looking for to introduce Protestant ideas into the church. It was ordered that Communion be administered in both kinds (i.e., both the bread and the wine), and clergy were allowed to marry. Cranmer had been secretly married for some time, and he now brought his wife over from Holland. Several resistant bishops were arrested and held in prison until Edward's death in 1553.

One of the most significant events of Edward's reign was the introduction in 1549 of the first Book of Common Prayer, which every church in England was required to use. It was a magnificent liturgical and literary achievement. Cranmer had a Calvinist (Presbyterian) view of the Eucharist, but he knew that the Prayer Book would not be accepted if he tried to introduce that line of thinking, so the book reflects a purely Catholic Eucharistic theology.[11] Three years later the Protestants had gained significant power in England, and a new version was introduced. The 1552 Prayer Book was a peculiarly Protestant document. When it was released neither Parliament nor the Convoca-

---

10. Henry had three more wives, Anne of Cleves (a marriage unconsummated and annulled), Catherine Howard (executed for committing adultery before and during her marriage, probably guilty), and Catherine Parr (who survived him). None produced children or had any significant effect on the church or the state.

11. Calvin taught that Christ's presence in the Eucharist is purely spiritual, and many Presbyterian leaders taught that his presence is dependent upon the faith of the believer (the doctrine of receptionism). The Catholic view, which is that of Anglicanism, is that Christ is objectively present in the elements of bread and wine, and only the benefit of receiving him is dependent upon faith.

tion of Bishops had even seen it, let alone approved it. It expressed the Catholic faith in the most Protestant language possible, and had a distinctly receptionist (Presbyterian) overtone. In 1553 Cranmer published the Forty-Two Articles of Religion, a statement of the doctrine of the Church in England.

In 1553 Edward died, having named his Protestant cousin Lady Jane Grey as his heir. Just before her coronation her father rather stupidly launched a rebellion to support her claim to the throne. This was taken by Parliament to be an act of treason, and they accused Jane of being a conspirator in it. Jane, her husband, and her father were condemned and executed. Mary, Henry VIII's daughter by Catherine of Aragon, became queen. She immediately restored papal rule to the church in England. She was welcomed by the people, who were sick of the regents' greed and of the attempts to force Protestantism on them, and who had loved her mother, Catherine. Mary's obsession with forcing absolute submission to the pope, however, turned the people against her. She imprisoned all who had led the Reformation, and executed most of them, including Thomas Cranmer. She slaughtered all who opposed her religion and her intention of placing a Spanish prince on England's throne. This bloodbath earned her the epithet "Bloody Mary." Her blind intolerance and her love of everything Spanish[12] brought about such a hatred for Roman Catholicism in England that for over 150 years after her death, any attempt to restore papal rule there was fiercely resisted.

Upon Mary's death in 1558 Henry VIII's last child, Elizabeth, the daughter of Anne Boleyn, became queen. She was every bit her father's daughter — superbly capable, highly intelligent, and, like him, evil-tempered, ruthless, and selfish. Her years under Edward and Mary, however, had taught her patience and self-control. She was a gifted diplomat and a wise and just ruler. She recognized that the people wanted neither the Roman Catholicism of Mary nor the Protestantism of Edward. Her first act when Parliament reconvened in 1559 was to pass the Act of Supremacy. This placed her as head of the English church, which from that time on has been known as the Church of En-

12. Her love of Spain was understandable. She was the granddaughter of Ferdinand and Isabella, and she and her mother had been rejected and humiliated by Henry.

gland. She refused, however, to use her father's title of Supreme Head of the Church, and no English monarch has taken it since. She immediately set about appointing bishops and revising the Forty-Two Articles of Religion, which were finally reduced to thirty-nine and released in 1571.[13] These are still considered a valid summary of Anglican doctrine, although it requires significant historical and theological background to interpret them correctly. She authorized a revision of the 1552 Prayer Book, removing the strictly Protestant parts and correcting the liturgy, and released the result as the 1559 Prayer Book.

Rome made several attempts to convince Elizabeth to return England to Roman Catholicism, but to no avail. Finally in 1570 Pope Pius V excommunicated her, confirming the breach between the Roman Catholic and Anglican churches. During the forty-five years of Elizabeth's reign, the Church of England produced a series of brilliant theologians and liturgists who laid a firm foundation for today's worldwide Anglican communion. There were brief attempts to restore Roman Catholicism or Protestantism, but none posed any significant threat to the stability of the now firmly established Church of England. Elizabeth died in 1603. Her reign was nothing less than resplendent, climaxing in the English Renaissance — the age of Spenser, Shakespeare, and Bacon — and establishing England as one of the most powerful nations on earth.

Great Britain and the Church of England had many ups and downs in the following centuries, including the eleven-year Puritan dictatorship of the Cromwells. By the end of Elizabeth's reign, however, Anglicanism as a unique expression of Catholic belief had been defined, and had taken its place among the world's leading Christian faiths.

The Anglican Communion

The Anglican communion is the worldwide brotherhood of all the churches in communion with the Church of England — those bodies, in other words, whose theology and liturgy are in essential agreement with that church, and which are for the most part descendants of it.

---

13. The Thirty-Nine Articles may be seen in the 1979 Prayer Book on pages 867-76, in the "Historic Documents" section.

Until the beginning of the twentieth century most Anglican churches were found in countries over which at one time or another the British flag had flown; but since at various times Great Britain influenced or ruled in almost every corner of the world, that amounted to a vast number of countries.

As the British Empire and the Church of England grew, it became evident that just as size destroyed the Roman Empire and inhibited the Roman Catholic Church, so it would threaten the Church of England. For this reason the policy evolved that governs the Anglican communion today: each country or region would have its own autonomous church (the Episcopal Church is one of these). Each church is free to control its own doctrine and practice along the same democratic lines that are followed in the Church of England. Each is recognized by the body of all the rest as a member of the Anglican communion as long as it remains within certain basic traditional doctrinal parameters. There is no written agreement or constitution other than a loyalty to the principles declared in the several Books of Common Prayer of the individual churches, all of which are based on that of the Church of England. Every ten years the Lambeth Conference (named after the archbishop's palace) is convened in England. This is a conference of Anglican bishops from all over the world, who discuss issues facing the church and try to come to some agreement on how to deal with them. This conference has a powerful influence on its member churches, although it has no real legal authority. The archbishop of Canterbury, likewise, has no authority outside of the Church of England, yet his influence throughout the Anglican communion is enormous. The binding force in the Anglican communion is almost mystical. It is nothing more than an understood mutual loyalty to Anglican traditions, yet its power to cement the communion together is prodigious. To Anglicans this is proof of the operation of the Holy Spirit in the church.

A unique characteristic of the Anglican Reformation was that the first Anglican theologians and church leaders made no attempt to establish a specific body of unified theology and liturgy. In fact, they avoided this, trusting in the promise of the Holy Spirit that he would lead the church into truth, but recognizing that in this process Christians would often err and stumble. Rome and the emerging Protestant denominations maintained that they were the only true church. The Anglican leaders were not willing to claim that the other churches were false. They believed that there is some truth to be found in all sincere attempts to fathom the Absolute Truth, and that the duty of Christians is to trust the Holy Spirit to help them discern it. There are certain parameters within which churches must remain in order to be considered in communion with the rest of Anglicanism, but within these parameters there is great freedom. Among the necessary beliefs are an acceptance of the historic episcopate and threefold ministry as essential, belief that the Bible contains all things necessary for salvation, belief in and use of the two major sacraments of baptism and the Eucharist, acceptance of the doctrines of the Apostles', Nicene, and Athanasian Creeds, and assent to the spirit and principles of the Thirty-Nine Articles of Religion.[14]

The byword of Anglicanism is *via media*, "the middle road." Anglicans emphasize that this does not mean *medium viae*, "the middle of the road," which implies a lack of commitment. *Via media* implies that the church seeks to retain the best of the teachings and practices of the Roman Catholic heritage but enrich them with the best of Protestant thought and custom. After the middle of the nineteenth century the influence of the Oxford movement led to a restoration of a strong emphasis within Anglicanism on ancient Catholic theology and liturgy. The church veered away from the Protestant doctrine of *sola Scriptura*, "the Bible alone," which allows doctrine to be derived from no other source than the Bible. Anglicanism looks to the Bible, human reason, and tradition equally for the affirmation of doctrine. The Oxford movement tended to polarize many parts of Anglicanism into "high church" and "low church" groups, but the extremes on either end represented only a small minority of Anglicans.[15] Lutheranism and East-

14. These may be modified within reason to fit any special conditions of the individual national church. For example, Article XXXVII in the Episcopal Church recognizes duly elected or appointed civil authority, whereas in England it acknowledges the authority of the monarch and Parliament.

15. In the early days "high church" and "low church" had nothing to do with liturgy or ceremony. "High churchmen" meant Tories, who were loyal to the king and accepted him as supreme head of the church; "low churchmen" were Whigs, whose loyalty was to Parliament. Since in the Tudor and Stuart dynasties the monarchs were faithful to the ancient traditions and Parliament was heavily influenced by Puritans and Presbyterians, the conflict came to be associated with a rich liturgical tradition versus a plain one.

ern Orthodoxy are the only other major non-Roman churches that greatly value early liturgical and doctrinal tradition.

A fiercely defended mainstay of Anglicanism is a belief in the "historic episcopate" or "apostolic succession."[16] Bishops of the historic episcopate can trace their consecration by the physical laying on of hands[17] through history in an unbroken line back to apostolic times. While the written records of many of these lines have been lost in the mists of history, there is little doubt that the succession is there and unbroken — this belief has been too highly treasured by all branches of Catholicism for there to be any doubt that it has been carefully observed. In fact, this is the grounds on which the Roman Catholic Church rejects the validity of Anglican clergy and thus of Anglican sacraments. For a sacrament to be valid, not only must all the outward forms be observed, but there must also be a proper "intention" — the administrator and recipient of the sacrament must intend to do as the outward signs indicate. The first bishop consecrated as an Anglican was Matthew Parker (1504-75), who was consecrated archbishop of Canterbury when Elizabeth I ascended the throne in 1558. Rome claims that since the English church was in heresy and schism, the succession was broken because there was no intention to consecrate a valid Catholic bishop.[18] The historic episcopate is the primary earthly evidence of the church's continuity with its apostolic origins. It is the means by which the sacramental structure of the church is preserved, and it is the sole guarantee of the devolution of authority from Jesus Christ to the church through his apostolic representatives (the bishops). For these reasons Catholicism (including Anglicanism) deems

16. This is one of the critical doctrinal differences between Anglicanism and Lutheranism. Most Lutherans have no strong objection to the concept of the historic episcopate, but do not require it or particularly value it. (An exception is the Swedish Lutheran Church, with which Anglicanism is in full communion. They require the historic episcopate, as Anglicanism does.)

17. The physical contact is required simply as an outward and visible sign of the continuity. There is no concept that the validity of a consecration actually depends on it — that would be "magic," and totally unacceptable to Christianity.

18. A story known as the "Nag's Head Fable" was circulated and believed for years. It told that Parker was consecrated in a mock ceremony in the Nag's Head Tavern by having ale poured over his head. This was nonsense, of course, but the story served for almost three centuries as powerful propaganda against the validity of the Church of England.

the historic episcopate to be essential to the very nature of the church. The teaching for millennia has been, "No bishop, no church." This has been one of the primary obstacles in ecumenical discussion with the Protestant bodies, most of whom place no value on the historic episcopate, and some of whom reject it out of hand. The historic episcopate has always had its challengers, but it is the consensus of the vast majority of Anglican theologians that it is essential to the church's being. There are two predominant Protestant polities in opposition to the episcopalian (bishop) polity of Catholicism: the presbyterian, which places all ecclesiastical authority in a single body, the "elders" (pastors or presbyters); and the congregational, which places all authority in the laity, and has no sacramental clergy (ministers are simply specially trained lay leaders).

Anglicanism distinguishes itself from both Roman Catholicism and Protestantism in its view of the role of Holy Scripture in the formulation of dogma (basic required beliefs). Roman Catholicism teaches that all doctrine was revealed at Pentecost in what is called "the deposit of faith," and that thereafter the authority to interpret that revelation has been the prerogative of the church. The faith is preserved by tradition, which is the primary source of the understanding of doctrine. Rome teaches that since the Bible was validated by the church, not the church by the Bible, tradition weighs more heavily than the Bible in the formulation of dogma. (But tradition cannot, of course, contradict anything taught in the Bible.) Protestantism, on the other hand, almost universally accepts the doctrine of *sola Scriptura*, "only the Bible."[19] This teaches that the Bible was given by God as the rule and guide to the Christian faith, and thus no doctrine is acceptable that is not clearly stated in it; in most of Protestantism (Lutheranism is an exception), tradition and nonscriptural revelation are not highly re-

19. The Bible consists of sixty-six books, thirty-nine of the Old Testament and twenty-seven of the New. The Jews translated their sacred scriptures into Greek in the third century BCE, producing a work known as the Septuagint, which included what we call the Old Testament plus fourteen other books. These fourteen and one other (II Esdras) are known as the Apocrypha ("Hidden"). They include such books as Tobit, Esther, and the Wisdom of Solomon. Eleven of these books are accepted as canonical by the Roman Church. All fifteen are rejected by Protestantism. In Anglicanism the Apocrypha may be used in worship and for study and meditation, but may not be considered in the formulation of doctrine.

garded.[20] Anglicanism, again following the *via media,* believes that the Bible contains all things necessary for salvation — no doctrine or practice is necessary beyond what is taught or commanded in the Bible — but nonscriptural doctrines and practices are perfectly acceptable as enrichment. For a doctrine to be considered essential it must be traditional (believed by a significant part of the church from the beginning), reasonable, and clearly stated in the Bible.

A document unique to Anglicanism is the Book of Common Prayer. This is not in fact a single document — every autonomous national Anglican church is free to produce its own Book of Common Prayer in its own language. All are based on that of the Church of England, however, and all are amazingly similar in structure and content. There has never been a Book of Common Prayer, from 1549 until today, that has not been controversial. Today's major prayer-book controversy lies in the fact that in recent years some Anglican churches, particularly the Episcopal Church, have included alternative versions of the Eucharist and principal offices that are very different from the traditional forms of 1549. These forms (such as the Episcopal Church's "Rite II" Eucharist) are valid and historically sound, but are based on different ancient sources than were used by Cranmer in 1549. Most churches, including the Church of England, have offered these in separate books of alternative services in order to preserve the integrity and historic continuity of the Book of Common Prayer. Many liturgiologists fear that offering alternatives in the primary prayer book will adulterate its historic validity. In America this controversy has produced much tension and has even led to schism.

Three creeds summarize the Anglican faith: the Apostles', Nicene, and Athanasian Creeds. All three are used in almost all Christian denominations, though the Apostles' Creed is by far the most commonly used in Protestantism. While it is almost never used liturgically, one of the most treasured by Anglicans is the Athanasian Creed, which is a virtually complete summary of the Catholic faith focusing on the doc-

20. Some Protestant denominations accept the Bible literally, believing that God dictated it word for word. The majority believe that the writers of the Bible were inspired by God and guided in their writings, but were subject to human error. This means that there are no false teachings that could in any way threaten the salvation of any person, but that there can be unimportant errors (discrepancies of dates and names, minor contradictions, and the like).

trine of the Trinity.[21] In the Anglican tradition the Nicene Creed is usually used in Eucharistic worship, and the Apostles' Creed in most other services.

Along with almost all of Christianity, Anglicanism steadfastly affirms the two major sacraments, holy Baptism and Holy Communion (the Holy Eucharist), as necessary to salvation.[22] The five minor sacraments — holy confirmation, holy orders (ordination), holy matrimony, holy penance (confession), and holy unction (the anointing of the sick), are freely accepted and practiced, but are not required. They are called "minor" because while they are rooted in the New Testament, they are not specifically commanded by Christ as the major sacraments are. Most Protestant groups see them as mere symbolic rituals, and some consider their elevation as sacraments "popish" and anti-Christian.

Anglicans (like many other Christians, including Catholics, the Eastern Orthodox, Lutherans, and many other Protestants) practice infant baptism, justifying it on both historic and theological grounds. The Bible tells of baptizing whole households, and there is no mention of the exclusion of infants. Another argument for infant baptism is that the grace of salvation cannot be earned — it is a free gift of God freely given and is in no way dependent upon the intention or righteousness of the recipient. This being the case, Anglicans see no reason to withhold baptism from an infant simply because he is incapable of deciding for himself. (The sacrament of confirmation is the time when the individual makes his own conscious commitment to Christ.)

The Holy Eucharist is the central act of Anglican worship and is the most sacred event of all Catholic spirituality. Unlike the Protestants (with the exception of most Lutherans), Anglicans believe that the glorified Christ is objectively present in the Blessed Sacrament — his presence is not a function of the faith of the recipient. Even if a nonbeliever

21. There is a reason it is not used liturgically. While it is a magnificent work, it is extremely long, and theologically recondite. It may be found in the 1979 Book of Common Prayer beginning on page 864.

22. When we say that something is necessary to salvation, this is not to imply that a person not accepting it is automatically damned. The promise of salvation is given to those who accept and live by the gospel. Anyone who has not heard the gospel or who has heard a corrupted version of it cannot be condemned for rejecting it. Also, it is God's judgment, not ours, as to the destiny of those who for whatever reason are outside the promise.

receives the Sacrament, he is receiving the body and blood of the risen and ascended Christ. Any benefit received is dependent on the recipient's faith and good intention, but the presence of Christ is not. Anglican Eucharistic theology differs from Roman in several points, among which two are critical: (1) Rome sees the Mass as a continuation of the sacrifice of Christ, while Anglicanism sees it as a commemoration of it; and (2) while both accept the objective presence of Christ in the Sacrament, Rome affirms the doctrine of transubstantiation (an explanation of how Christ is present), while Anglicanism simply accepts the mystery, refusing any attempt to explain it.

For all of these reasons, Anglicanism can be said to represent the *via media*, the "middle road." Like Lutheranism, it attempts to embody the best of reformed Catholicism and inspired Protestant thought.

THE REFORMED CHURCHES

The Reformed churches all have a common origin in sixteenth-century Reformation Switzerland, the home of Calvinism, the theology of which they all share. Most of the churches that we now call Reformed are rooted in the Continental movement (whereas Presbyterianism, a related faith, is based more on Scottish Calvinism). Although the impetus for the Protestant Reformation came from Martin Luther (1483-1536), Reformed theology draws more on the teachings of the Czech Jan Hus (1372?-1417), the Swiss Huldreich Zwingli (1484-1531), and the French John Calvin (1509-64).

The Hussite movement, known as the Unity of Brethren, became very strong in Hungary and Bohemia, and spread through eastern Europe as far north as Poland. Despite centuries of persecution by Roman Catholicism, various Protestant groups, and most recently Communism, it still survives today in the regions around the Czech Republic. Most of the Hussites, however, placed less emphasis on the teachings of Huss, instead embracing Zwingli's and Calvin's teachings as they began to spread.

In the sixteenth century, Calvinism spread to France, where its adherents came to be known as Huguenots.[1] In 1559 they established a presbyterian form of organization, as opposed to the congregational form espoused in Eastern Europe. The Huguenots are probably best

---

1. The name originally referred to a dissident political movement led by Bezanson Hugues.

118

remembered as the victims of the Saint Bartholomew's Day Massacre. On August 24, 1572, under the urging of the queen mother Catherine de Medici, over fifty thousand Huguenots were slaughtered in Paris and the provinces. They, like other Reformed groups throughout Europe, suffered persecution for two more centuries. In 1685 Louis XIV revoked the limited toleration allowed the Huguenots, and at least 250,000 French Protestants emigrated to Germany, Holland, England, and America. Meanwhile, the Reformed movement spread from France into Italy and Iberia, and still represents the preponderance of Protestants in those regions. In 1800 Napoleon placed them under state control and put their pastors on state salary. This did not end in France until 1905.

In Germany, the Peace of Westphalia[2] in 1648 legalized the Reformed Church in any German province whose prince approved it. Nonetheless an attempt was made in the Rhineland a few years later to wipe it out. Many fled to the Netherlands, America, and Protestant Prussia, where Reformed churches were established and tolerated. In 1609 the Hohenzollern Elector of Brandenburg was converted to Calvinism. Thereafter the church flourished in Prussia. In 1817 King Friedrich Wilhelm III proposed to unite the Reformed and Lutheran churches. Many Lutherans and Reformed Protestants did not join in the union, but it nevertheless took place and became a model of Christian unity for most German Protestants. In 1884 a Reformed Alliance was organized to preserve the Reformed heritage. In 1934 this Alliance drew up a formal protest against the Nazi *Führerprinzip,* the "Führer Principle" that had named Hitler as the supreme head of all the churches in Germany. This alliance led to the Barmen Synod later that year, in which Lutheran, United, and Reformed leaders drew up the "Barmen Declaration," stating that Jesus Christ is the only authority in the church. This evolved into the "Confessing Church," which resisted Hitler throughout his reign and led to the martyrdom of many Christians, the most notable of whom was Dietrich Bonhoeffer. After the war the Confessing Church disappeared, but the Reformed Alliance still remains active throughout Germany.

In England in 1648 the Puritans attempted to have Presbyterianism

2. This treaty ended the Thirty Years' War. This war between Roman Catholics and Protestants was one of the bloodiest and most destructive conflicts in history.

become the established church, but their efforts failed. The king and the Church of England were restored to power in 1660. The "Glorious Revolution" of 1688 expelled the Roman Catholic King James II, thus allowing limited toleration of all "nonconformists," including the Reformed churches. In Scotland, the Anglican bishops refused to acknowledge the legitimacy of William and Mary. They were therefore granted no influence in the government, and as a result Presbyterianism became the established Church of Scotland. In Ireland, neither Anglicanism nor Protestantism ever gained a significant foothold in the firmly Roman Catholic southern portions ("The Irish Free State"), but they both became strong in the north, particularly in Ulster ("Northern Ireland").

Throughout the history of the Reformed movement the Netherlands was a haven of tolerance for many religious dissidents. Reformed Christians often fled there during the many persecutions in Europe. The end of the Thirty Years' War brought independence to the Netherlands, and by that time the Reformed church had become associated with Dutch nationalism. It flourished, even under Napoleonic attempts to control it, and Dutch Reformed churches are still strong in America and throughout the many parts of the world where the Dutch colonized and traded for two centuries.

In America, many of those who shaped the political and religious standards of the colonies were members of Reformed churches. The American Reformed movement was characterized for the most part by rigorous discipline and the strictest adherence to Calvinist principles. Its followers believed that constructive activity was holy, while idle enjoyment was sinful. Art, music, and literature were acceptable only if spiritually edifying. Rest and refreshment were justified only as the means of restoring strength so that one could continue labor, or to allow time to pray and study Scripture. The so-called "Protestant work ethic" was a Reformed characteristic. Some humorist once observed that American Reformed Christians lived with a constant gnawing fear that somewhere in the world someone might be happy. The hallmarks of a Christian society, the Reformed argued, were saving souls and social improvement. Reformed churches were in the vanguard of abolitionism, temperance, and women's suffrage. After the Civil War and even into modern times, the Reformed movement has been torn by many theological disagreements, among which are evolution versus creationism, and biblical criticism versus literalism.

120

Reformed churches, in keeping with the belief of Calvin, consider themselves to be the Roman Catholic Church Reformed. They argue that the papal church abrogated its validity by its theological and moral corruption. In his *Institutes of the Christian Religion,* Calvin referred to the Roman Catholic Church as "the Mother of all the godly." Of the traditional teachings, he rejected only those he considered contrary to or unsupported by Holy Scripture. Members of the Reformed churches believe in justification by faith alone (not by good works) and in the Bible as the sole source of doctrine. (A more in-depth look at these beliefs can be found in the chapter on Presbyterianism.)

Only the two major sacraments of baptism and Communion are accepted. In the Eucharist, all reference to the sacrifice of the Mass is rejected. There is disagreement about the presence of Christ. Some accept Zwingli's teaching of receptionism, which teaches that Christ's presence in the Sacrament is wholly dependent upon the faith of the believer. Others share to some extent with Lutherans and the several Catholic churches the doctrine of the real presence. This teaches that the resurrected Christ is present, regardless of the faith of the believer, but that the spiritual benefit derived from the sacrament is a function of that faith. Calvin, however, diverged from Catholic teaching in that he denied that the actual resurrected body of Jesus is present. He maintained that Christ's presence is purely spiritual. In Reformed churches, the Eucharist is celebrated at a simple table (never called an altar), and the congregation either gathers around the table or passes the elements of the Eucharist from person to person in the pews.

There is also disagreement about the doctrine of predestination. All believe in "positive predestination," that God chooses an "elect," those who are predestined to be saved; the rest may or may not be saved, depending on their choices in life. Many also believe in "double predestination," that there are some predestined to "reprobation," who will be damned regardless of how they live. This was Calvin's teaching, but it is rejected by many Reformed groups.

Most Reformed Christians believe in the policy originally posited in the Swiss Reformation — namely, that church and state should render service to each other yet remain distinct. They believe that there should be a reciprocal relationship of noninterfering mutual support between church and state. This is the true meaning of the phrase "separation of church and state," which was never meant to imply that the church and the state should be at odds with one another. Obedience is required even to unworthy rulers, except when the ruler commands disobedience to God. Even then, however, active resistance or rebellion is forbidden — it is the responsibility of political officials, not the church, to bring the government into line. This principle was blatantly disregarded in the English Civil War, which resulted in the murder of King Charles I.[3] Many colonial Reformed churches refused to support the American Revolution even though they were in sympathy with the cause (although they did not object to their members fighting for it, as long as they did not do so in the name of the church). Today there are some nations that have an established Reformed church (such as the Church of Scotland), but there is little difference in practice and beliefs between these and the free Reformed churches. While these churches are established, it is tacitly understood that they do not meddle in politics, and the government does not attempt to define theology or worship.

Reformed churches were among the first to use the vernacular in their liturgy. They removed everything that even hinted at the sacrifice of the Mass. They did not consider confession to be a sacrament, but they regularly practiced it as a spiritual discipline. Auricular confession (to an individual) was very rare, but congregational confession was a common event. The singing of psalms was a central part of the liturgy, and to this day music is an important part of Reformed worship. Most Reformed churches offer a wide variety of musical types, but some still restrict singing to the psalms. Preaching is basic to Reformed worship, and in the early days several hours of preaching on Sunday was the norm. In recent years most Reformed worship has been considerably modernized, with an increased interest in using the arts in worship, and with the use of contemporary inclusive language. There is also a vastly increased concern for social needs and responsibilities.

The modern values of the Reformed churches have also led to a recognition of the need for a well-educated clergy and a well-informed

---

3. While the Civil War and the overthrow of Charles Stuart were done allegedly in the name of Parliament and the people, there is little question that the real purpose was the replacement of the Church of England with either the Presbyterian (Reformed) Church or with Puritanism.

laity. In the early days the clergy used to gather regularly for discussion and mutual learning. Today they are carefully trained in accredited universities and seminaries. The training of the laity in earlier days was accomplished by preaching and teaching the catechism. Today that training is done through Sunday schools that use curricula developed by educational experts, and by relating the faith to the daily life of the people.

In 1934 the Evangelical and Reformed Church was organized by a merger of the Reformed Church in the United States and the Evangelical Synod of North America. Their doctrine and practice was a combination of Calvinist Reformed thinking and that of several conservative Lutheran traditions. In 1957 this group merged with the General Council of Congregational Christian Churches to form the United Church of Christ.[4] This was an unusual union, because of the presbyterian form of government of the ERC and the congregational form of the GCCCC.

Despite the various mergers, there are still several independent Reformed and Presbyterian groups in America, especially in areas that have large German, Dutch, or Scandinavian populations. The largest and probably best known is the Reformed Church in America, commonly called the Dutch Reformed Church.

While the influence of Zwingli and Calvin is felt throughout Christianity, it is best preserved in the teachings of the worldwide Reformed churches.

---

4. See the chapter on the United Church of Christ for a more thorough discussion of its teachings.

THE MENNONITES

The term "Mennonite" refers to a large number of similar but separate groups, all descended from the sixteenth-century Anabaptists and named for Menno Simons, a Dutch priest who originally organized the movement. Today Mennonites are found worldwide, with over 2,600 congregations in North America representing 260,000 members,[1] and even larger numbers abroad.

The Anabaptists were an early Reformation movement known as the "Swiss Brethren." They first organized in 1525 in Zurich, Switzerland, led by Konrad Grebel and a group of religious dissidents who maintained that Luther and Zwingli had not gone far enough in their reforms. They rejected infant baptism and denied any significance to the Mass other than as a memorial reenactment of the Last Supper. Because of their rejection of Roman Catholic doctrine they were often persecuted and martyred. They were contemporary with Zwingli, although the first Anabaptist leaders were younger than he.

The name "Anabaptist" was originally a derisive label, but the Swiss Brethren later used it themselves. It means "re-baptizer," alluding to their re-baptism of those who had been baptized as infants. The Anabaptists' main emphasis, like the Calvinists' and Lutherans', was a belief in personal responsibility to God and the sole authority of Scripture as a source of doctrine. Unlike those groups, however, the Anabaptists were pacifists and were firmly opposed to state churches.

---

1. 1995 Yearbook of the National Council of Churches of Christ in the USA.

Many practiced communalism,[2] the equal sharing of all resources and responsibilities. Because most Anabaptist communities were very small, the system worked for them, whereas it eventually failed in all the larger faiths. The Puritans, for example, at first attempted communalism in England and in New England, but soon abandoned it as unproductive. Among the Anabaptists, failure to meet one's moral, theological, and social responsibilities could result in the "ban," by which a sinner was ostracized, cast out, and in some cases rebuffed as if he were dead. This soon became controversial, however, eventually resulting in schism. Today only the most conservative Mennonite groups practice the ban (which they usually call "shunning").

Anabaptism appealed primarily to the uneducated lower classes, and was thus held in contempt not only by the ecclesiastical and political aristocracy, but also by the better-educated mainstream Protestant reformers. As a result, Anabaptists were suppressed and persecuted from all sides. Many Anabaptist communities withdrew from mainstream life and fled into the country where they lived in what today would be called communes.

In 1492 Menno Simons was born in Friesland, a region now shared between Germany and the Netherlands. He was ordained a Roman Catholic priest in 1515, and served as pastor in his hometown until 1536. In January of that year he renounced his Roman Catholic ties and joined the Anabaptists. He gathered together the many scattered Anabaptists in northern Europe, organizing and teaching them. His followers soon took his name, calling themselves Mennonites. With the death of many of the Anabaptist leaders from persecution and in the Peasants' War, Simons somewhat reluctantly fell into a position of leadership of the movement. He organized and institutionalized the dozens of independent Anabaptist communities and brought together the widely scattered individuals. In spite of persecution, the group flourished and grew. Simons established congregations all over Holland and northwestern Germany, but most of the Dutch communities dwindled or fell away.

In 1554, because of a dispute over the principles of the ban, the Dutch Mennonites divided into "Flemings" and "Waterlanders." The

2. This was an equitable sharing of labor and resources. It should not be confused with the Communism of Marx and his disciples.

former, due to constant disagreements, eventually all but disappeared, there being only a handful left in Holland today. The Waterlanders were also fragmented, but in 1811 they united, dropped the name Mennonite, and called themselves *Doopsgezinde* ("Baptist Persuasion"), the name by which they are known today. The Mennonites flourished in Germany, and in 1788 the promise of land and exemption from military conscription lured thousands of German Mennonites to Russia. They settled there, although they retained their German language and culture. In 1860 a small group felt a call to a more disciplined life, and founded the Mennonite Brethren Church. They thrived until the 1870s, when the Tsar required that all Russians, including the pacifist Mennonites, serve in the military. Also, the Cossacks began persecuting Jews and all Christians who were not Russian Orthodox. Huge numbers of Mennonites left for America, settling mostly in the Midwest. In 1918 Soviet oppression forced the rest underground, and their numbers dwindled greatly. Since the fall of Communism they have begun to grow again.

Persecution of Mennonites in western Europe continued well into the eighteenth century. The Netherlands, Germany, and Alsace were more tolerant of religious dissidents than most other European areas, so many fled to those areas. Large numbers also emigrated to America. In most European countries the professions were legally closed to the Mennonites (as they were to the Jews), so their primary source of income was either farming or business and banking. As a result many became quite wealthy and began to have considerable financial influence in the cities. They were attracted to the intellectual revolution known as the Enlightenment and produced large numbers of artists, writers, musicians, and promoters of social reform. By the end of the eighteenth century the persecutions had ended, and the Mennonites had achieved respect for their honesty and industry. Paradoxically, with this new acceptance by society, their numbers began to drop markedly. By 1850 there were only about a tenth as many Mennonites in the Netherlands as there had been in 1700.[3]

---

3. Throughout history, persecuted groups have often prospered most under the cruellest periods of their persecution. Christianity thrived under Roman persecution. It has been said that the unkindest blow that ever fell on Christianity was its legalization in the Roman Empire in the fourth century.

A major schism took place in Switzerland and southern Germany in 1693-97. The chief elder or "bishop" of Switzerland, Jakob Ammann, left the established Mennonites to form a new community dedicated to preserving biblical discipline and ancient Christian values. Ammann was influenced by the Lutheran Pietist movement, which emphasized personal religious experience and simplicity of life. For example, the Pietists used hooks and eyes instead of buttons, because in eighteenth-century Europe fancy buttons were a symbol of status and wealth. Ammann's followers renounced all modern conveniences, describing themselves as "plain people." Almost all supported themselves by farming. They called themselves Old Order Amish Mennonites, after Ammann's name, but are usually simply called Amish.[4] Many Amish migrated to America, most settling in Pennsylvania and the Midwest.[5] Most are trilingual — in religious services they speak pure Hanoverian German; at home they speak a corrupted dialect of *Hochdeutsch* (Southern German) called "Pennsylvania Dutch";[6] and with their non-Amish neighbors they speak English. They worship in homes rather than in churches. Today they are the second largest of the Mennonite groups, with 898 communities representing 81,000 members.

The first major Mennonite migrations to America had taken place in 1663, when Mennonites came here for freedom to exercise their religion and in order to escape European military conscription.[7] Most of those who came were German-speaking, and they retained their language as a symbol of the origins of their faith and to insulate them from the corruption that might come from their "nonbelieving" neighbors. Their main desire was to be left alone to worship and work as they pleased. They took their pacifism seriously. In a 1775 statement to the Pennsylvania Assembly, refusing to participate in the Revolutionary Army, they said,

4. The name is pronounced "AH-mish" with a broad *a*, not "AY-mish" with a long *a*.

5. A rather good view of Amish life can be seen in the film *Witness* with Harrison Ford, Kelly McGillis, and Lukas Haas.

6. It is not really Dutch, but *Deutsch*, German.

7. While various Mennonite groups have many theological and disciplinary differences, they universally agree on pacifism. They believe that there is no justification for killing another human being under any circumstances.

It is our principle to feed the hungry and give the thirsty drink; we have dedicated ourselves to serve all men in everything that can be helpful to the preservation of men's lives, but we find no freedom in giving, or doing, or assisting in anything by which men's lives are destroyed or hurt.

In 1783 they were accused of treason for feeding starving British soldiers. During the Civil War, when both sides had mandatory conscription, most Mennonites hired substitutes or paid an exemption fee of three hundred dollars (five hundred in the South).[8] Those who fought were often excommunicated. In World Wars I and II Mennonite men were exempted from the military in exchange for serving in such positions as clerks or hospital orderlies.

In 1860 representatives of a number of independent Mennonite groups met in West Point, Iowa, to form a North American conference. Today it is known as the General Conference Mennonite Church. It consists of 224 congregations representing nearly 34,000 members. The largest group is known simply as the Mennonite Church, consisting of 1058 churches representing almost 96,000 people. There are also several other smaller conferences, and large numbers of independent congregations who do not believe in such organizations.

By the beginning of the twentieth century many Mennonites had become more modern in their approach, dropping their traditional use of German and instituting such mainstream practices as Sunday schools. This led to a number of divisions, and today there are several Mennonite groups, spanning a wide spectrum. Those on one end seem like liberal Baptists, while at the other extreme are the Hutterian Brethren (or "Hutterites"), an ultra-conservative group who still live in closed communities and practice common ownership of all goods. They originated in the sixteenth century in Moravia and the Tirol under the leadership of Jakob Hutter, who was eventually martyred. There are very few of these communities left in Europe, but about 6700 Hutterites are found in the upper Great Plains of North America.

---

8. This was legal at that time, and exercising it placed a considerable burden on the Mennonites. The law was passed mainly to allow the rich and powerful to escape service. Three hundred dollars was well over a year's wages for a farm hand or laborer.

During the most brutal periods of persecution in the sixteenth century, Anabaptists and Mennonites sought safety by withdrawing from mainstream society, trying to live quietly and avoid notice. In time this became a basic characteristic of their theology and daily practice, and they emphasize a separation of religion and the world. Some groups, such as the Hutterites and the Amish, shelter themselves as much as possible from society. They lead a very simple agrarian life, resisting the use of any technology not known in the sixteenth century.[9] They thus use no motorized farm machinery, yet many of them have become quite prosperous, and very few could be considered poor. The main reason for this prosperity is their strong sense of community — they willingly help one another and share their goods and labor whenever there is a need. The less strict groups also inculcate this sense of community, and this protects them from being corrupted by worldly temptations. They run businesses and sell services in mainstream society, taking pride in honesty, hard work, and quality of goods and services; to them these virtues have an important religious significance. This has earned them great respect in the communities in which they live, and people are anxious to hire them when possible.

Clothing standards vary greatly among congregations. Some groups, such as the Amish, wear almost a habit — the men wear dark trousers and a vest or jacket, a blue, gray, or white long-sleeved shirt, and a straw hat; women wear a simple dress with no "frills" (never shorts or slacks), and a cap or small bonnet. At the other end of the spectrum there is no standard other than that of simplicity and utility — showy or immodest clothing, jewelry, and pretentious hairdos are frowned upon. The more traditional Mennonite women wear a small black or white head covering to distinguish themselves as such. It is a custom among many Mennonite groups that the men are clean-shaven until they marry, and then grow a beard to show their unavailability. Most continue to shave their upper lip, however, because in Europe the moustache was a traditional symbol of the military, an institution of which Mennonites strongly disapprove.

Mennonites are Trinitarian, accepting Jesus Christ as the son of God

---

9. They are not rigidly opposed to new ideas or technology. If they determine that something new will enhance their life and will not interfere with the simplicity and objectives of their lives, they will adopt it.

and the Savior of mankind. They affirm the Bible as their sole authority for doctrine and as the primary guide to their way of life and work. They look to the structure of the apostolic church as their model for congregational standards and practices. They accept believer's baptism (never baptism for infants) as a ritual proclamation of their relationship to Christ. Baptism may be administered by affusion (pouring) or immersion, although immersion is less common among all but the most conservative groups. They consider Communion to be a reenactment and dramatization of the Last Supper, symbolic of Christ's sacrifice for our salvation, and Christ is not considered present in it. Communion is celebrated only annually or semi-annually in most Mennonite congregations and is often accompanied by foot-washing. Neither baptism nor Communion is considered a sacrament in the Catholic sense; they are, rather, looked upon as symbolic rituals. Most congregations practice pacifism and forbid the swearing of oaths, lawsuits, holding civil office, resistance to violence, and the bearing of arms, although these proscriptions are not universal. All have established disciplinary standards for their members, and these vary from the rather liberal to the very rigorous.

Worship services are liturgically very simple — almost austere — and are sermon-centered. Most congregations sing hymns and psalms, but musical instruments are usually forbidden. (Members are free to play instruments, but not in worship.) In recent years some congregations have experimented with new liturgical expressions similar to those found in the more traditional Protestant denominations, but this is not common.

Most congregations are joined into any of several conferences, although the Hutterites and Amish do not participate in any inter-congregational organizations. In all branches of Mennonites, however, congregations communicate with each other regularly and are usually very cooperative, especially when there is disaster or unusual need. They would also never hesitate to help non-Mennonites in distress. There is a Mennonite World Conference held every five years, but it is strictly for communication and mutual inspiration and support — it has no doctrinal or jurisdictional authority over any congregation or local conference.

Standards of education vary greatly between congregations. Many have their own schools, avoiding public schooling, although public schools are also commonly used. The more conservative not only refuse to use the public schools but also usually discourage education beyond the eighth grade (although few forbid it for those who show an aptitude and a desire for higher education). Most congregations and conferences, however, not only encourage higher education, but sponsor schools, universities, and seminaries to provide it.[10] In fact, the education level of American Mennonites is slightly above average.

In spite of centuries of persecution, the Mennonites have thrived as a faith for over 450 years, exemplifying discipline, strength of spirit, trust in God, and simplicity of life.

10. A 1972 Supreme Court decision granted Mennonites and related groups an exemption from states' mandatory education laws. They found that the eighth-grade education provided by the Mennonites is usually comparable or superior to the education provided by most public high schools by the legal quitting age.

THE PRESBYTERIANS

The Presbyterian church is a product of the Protestant Reformation of the sixteenth century. The name refers to presbyterianism, one of the three major systems of ecclesiastical polity (administrative structure).[1] Presbyterian polity is based on pastors (trained, ordained clergy) and "elders" (elected laity), who have joint, equal authority in decision-making.[2] Its structure ranges from the pastors and elders of local congregations up through various levels of regional and national assemblies.

There are several so-called "Presbyterian churches," all of which have common roots and are very similar in theology and practice.[3] Through the centuries they have seen a steady flow of schisms and

1. The other two are episcopalianism (government by bishops through the threefold ministry of bishops, priests, and deacons) and congregationalism (government by democratic vote of individual congregations). These words are not capitalized because they are the names of systems, not churches.

2. The name is derived from the Greek *presbyteros*, "elder." The word "priest" is derived from the same word, via the Vulgar Latin *prester*, from the late Latin *presbyter.*

3. The most important in America are (in order of size) the Presbyterian Church (U.S.A.) (PCUSA), the Presbyterian Church in America (PCA), the Cumberland Presbyterian Church, the Evangelical Presbyterian Church, the Associate Reformed Presbyterian Church (General Synod), the Korean Presbyterian Church in America, the Orthodox Presbyterian Church, and the Reformed Presbyterian Church of North America. The two largest of these are the PCUSA (4,000,000 members) and the PCA (240,000 members).

mergers because of differences or similarities of politics, theology, or mores. They all fall into a broad category of denominations, known as the "Reformed and Presbyterian churches," that are rooted in the teachings of Huldreich Zwingli and John Calvin[4] and include such groups as the United Church of Christ, the Dutch Reformed Church, the Reformed Church in America, and the several Presbyterian churches.

Theology and Practice

Presbyterianism is primarily based on the teachings of Zwingli and Calvin.[5] Another important influence on British (and thus American) Presbyterianism was the sixteenth-century Scot John Knox. During his exile under the Roman Catholic Mary Stuart ("Mary Queen of Scots"), he met Calvin in Geneva. Upon his return to Scotland in 1559 he led the movement for religious reform, and with the drafting of the *Confessions of Faith* in 1560 he brought about the establishment of Presbyterianism as the official religion of Scotland. Most of the Presbyterian missionaries to the colonies were Scots, and thus strongly influenced by Knox.

The early Reformed and Presbyterian churches considered themselves the Roman Catholic Church Reformed, and thus the only true church.[6] Calvin's *Institutes of the Christian Religion* (1536) refers to the Holy Catholic Church as the "Mother of all the godly." He believed that the Roman Church had abrogated its validity and authority by its corruption.

4. Born in France as Jean Cauvin, he was trained in law and theology. His main religious writing was done after he moved to Geneva, Switzerland, and wrote under the name of John Calvin.

5. Modern Presbyterianism focuses primarily on the doctrines of Calvin and John Knox, while Zwingli's teachings are more influential in the Reformed churches. Nevertheless, Zwingli has had an enormous influence on the modern Presbyterian churches, even though it is rarely noticed in discussions of their theology.

6. Most of the early Protestant groups believed that there could be only one true church, and each thought itself to be such. Anglicanism, on the other hand, believed that valid Christianity could be expressed in many ways within the parameters of Catholic tradition, including as Anglicanism, Roman Catholicism, Eastern Orthodoxy, and later even Lutheranism.

Presbyterianism is what is called a "confessional" church, committing itself to one or more formal statements of faith called "confessions."[7] A confession is more than a creed — it is a detailed exposition of theology and practice. Some of the more important Presbyterian confessions are Zwingli's Sixty-seven Articles (1523); the Zurich Consensus of 1543; the Second Helvetic Confession (which guided all Calvinist churches east of Switzerland); and the Westminster Confession, which had its greatest influence in the British Isles and is the primary confession of most Western Presbyterian churches.

As do most of the other Protestants, Presbyterians believe in justification by faith alone (not by good works), and in the Bible as the sole source of doctrine (sola Scriptura). To this they add the doctrine of Deo solo gloria ("Glory only to God"), which teaches that the Bible is the norm of faith, with no revelation beyond that which is in the Bible. This is heartily rejected by the Catholic churches, which teach that the church validated the Bible, not vice versa. At least as important for the Presbyterians is the triad of doctrines, sola Christus, sola gratias, sola fide ("Christ Alone, Grace Alone, Faith Alone"). These teach that salvation is a free gift of God's grace through Christ, and cannot be earned or merited. These teachings are wholly acceptable to traditional Catholicism, with perhaps one exception: Reformation teaching is that good works are a sign of faith and emanate from it, but can have absolutely no effect toward attaining salvation. Catholicism teaches that while this is true, it is also true that good works done for the purpose of doing God's will can develop and nurture stronger faith, which in turn leads to salvation. It is a slight, but important, difference.

Presbyterians encourage plain churches with a minimum of decoration. Their liturgy is simple, based primarily on scriptural readings, preaching, and hymns. In the early days, in order to avoid the complex music and ceremonial that had developed over the centuries in Roman Catholicism, the only acceptable music for worship was the singing of psalms. The Protestant churches no longer fear the threat of a "backslide" into Roman Catholicism, however, and many are thus much more comfortable with traditional forms than were the early reform-

7. This has nothing to do with confession as a recounting of one's sins, although the word comes from the same Latin root.

ers. This has led to a modern liturgical renewal, and to a greater appreciation of ancient traditions.

A key doctrinal issue of the Presbyterian churches is predestination. This is the teaching that God, before the creation, predetermined who would be saved. It is based on Romans 8:29-30: "For those whom he foreknew he also predestined to be conformed to the image of his Son, in order that he might be the first-born within a large family. And those whom he predestined he also called; and those whom he called he also justified; and those whom he justified he also glorified" (NRSV). Some Presbyterians accept only what can be called "positive predestination" — God predetermines who is to be saved, and leaves to their own devices all the rest. Some of the latter may find faith, and because of that be saved. The official teaching, however, is what is known as "double predestination" — God also predetermined who will be damned. This was the teaching of John Calvin. He said that while his reason found it appalling it was nevertheless scriptural, and he was not competent to judge the one who is the very standard of justice. His opponents argued that God wills that "not . . . one of these little ones should be lost" (Matt. 18:14, NRSV). Calvin did not deny free will — we are still free to make our own decisions — but he believed that the nature of our decisions is contingent upon our state of salvation.

The teachings of Jacobus Arminius rose in opposition to Calvin's interpretation. He taught that predestination would be a violation of God's gift of free will and that the omniscient God simply knows in advance what decisions we will make ("prescience" or foreknowledge rather than predetermination); God thus knows whether our choices will lead us to salvation or damnation. Fearing that Arminianism would lead the church back to "popery," the Synod of Dort in 1618 affirmed double predestination as orthodox theology for all Reformed and Presbyterian churches.[8]

---

8. "The fact that some receive from God the gift of faith within time, and that others do not, stems from his eternal decision. For all his works are known to God from eternity *(Acts 15:18; Eph. 1:11)*. In accordance with this decision he graciously softens the hearts, however hard, of his chosen ones and inclines them to believe, but by his just judgment he leaves in their wickedness and hardness of heart those who have not been chosen." *Council of Dordt, First Head of Doctrine of Divine Predestination, Article 5.*

Some Presbyterian and Reformed groups accept predestination in its strictest sense. The majority, however, interpret it more within the larger context of Calvin's teachings about grace. They see it as a sign of salvation rather than a criterion for it: "It is to be held as beyond all doubt that if you believe and are in Christ, you are elected."[9] The Westminster Confession says that predestination is to be "held in harmony with the doctrine of [God's] love to all mankind . . . [and] with the doctrine that God desires not the death of any sinner, but has provided in Christ a salvation sufficient for all."[10]

A form of predestination set forth in the writings of Saint Augustine and affirmed by Saint Thomas Aquinas was accepted by Luther and many Anglican theologians. It teaches that man's salvation is determined by an unmerited gift of God's grace, and is in that sense predestined. It also teaches God's reprobation of man's sin. The concept is similar to that proposed by Arminius.

Presbyterianism accepts only two sacraments, baptism and Communion. It also considers preaching to be an indispensable part of worship and one of the marks of the true Church. Thus in a truly Calvinist Presbyterian church the baptismal font, Communion table, and pulpit are all on the same physical level.[11] Early Presbyterians placed such an emphasis on preaching that the norm for Sunday worship included a two-hour sermon on the Old Testament in the morning, two hours on the New Testament in the afternoon, and a two-hour discussion of the two sermons in the evening. Worshipers were mandated to attend all three services.

Calvin wanted the Eucharist celebrated weekly, with recipients having made confession first. (He did not accept "auricular confession" — confession to a priest — but he expected communicants to make a self-examination and confess corporately or privately to God.)

---

9. Second Helvetic Confession, 5.059.

10. Amendment to the Westminster Confession of Faith, 6.192.

11. In Catholic churches, preaching is considered much less important than the sacraments. The Eucharist is considered the most sacred act, so the altar is always placed in the most honored position. The pulpit, while it may be physically elevated for the sake of acoustics, is placed in a "low" position. The baptismal font was traditionally placed at the entrance of the nave, symbolic of baptism as the entrance to the church. Most Catholic baptisms today, however, take place at the chancel steps, in front of the congregation.

He saw the Eucharist as a foretaste of the messianic banquet. Most of his followers thought it too sacred for frequent use, and today infrequent Eucharists are the norm. Some celebrate the Eucharist monthly, but most celebrate it quarterly and some even less frequently.

Zwingli taught that Christ is not present in the Eucharist, but that it is simply a memorial of him. Calvin, on the other hand, taught that Christ is present, but not in the elements of bread and wine.[12] He believed that Christ is present only spiritually through the faith of the worshipers. This is essentially the current Presbyterian belief.

Organization

The authority in individual congregations is shared between pastors (ordained clergy) and elders ("presbyters"), who are laity elected by the congregation. At the parish level this is called the session. The regional authority is the presbytery, which is made up of elected pastors and elders who serve specific terms. At the higher levels the government is comprised of the synods, and on the national level the general assembly. Ordination is not considered sacramental, but is the presbytery's formal recognition that one is adequately qualified and trained to serve as a pastor. In most Presbyterian groups pastors may be male or female.[13]

History

Presbyterian theology has its earliest roots in the fourth-century writings of Saint Augustine of Hippo, the first to offer a definition of predestination as he understood Saint Paul to mean it in Romans 8:29. Saints Bernard de Clairvaux (twelfth century) and Thomas Aquinas

12. It is up to the individual congregation whether wine or grape juice is used for the Eucharist. Since Presbyterians do not believe that Christ is objectively present in the elements, the specific nature of those elements is not particularly important.

13. Women are ordained in spite of John Knox's contempt for the sex. When Elizabeth I ascended the English throne in 1558, he wrote *The First Blast of the Trumpet Against the Monstrous Regiment of Women,* in which he described women as "weak, frail, impatient, feeble, foolish, . . . unconstant, variable, cruel, and lacking the spirit of counsel."

(thirteenth century) analyzed the concept further; their interpretations were (and still are) in complete accord with the teachings of Roman Catholicism.[14] Calvin's refinement of the doctrine, however, is a deviation from the original teaching of Augustine and is considered heresy by the Roman Catholic Church.

As the Reformation gained momentum in Europe, there developed three major centers of thought: Geneva,[15] where the disciples of Calvin gathered, Wittenberg, under Lutheran leadership, and Canterbury, where Roman Catholicism was evolving into Anglicanism. Even in those days Holland was liberal in its political and religious attitudes, and many reformers sought refuge in Amsterdam.

By the middle of the sixteenth century national Calvinist churches were beginning to form in Switzerland, Belgium, France, England, and (under John Knox) Scotland. By the time the Reformation was firmly established Calvin and Knox were the most important leaders of Presbyterianism worldwide.

In 1643 the British Parliament, dominated by Presbyterians, convened the Westminster Assembly to attempt to replace the Church of England. The Westminster Confession was formulated, and this statement of faith is a key confession for most Presbyterian bodies to this day.[16]

While the Puritans and "pilgrims" who came to Plymouth, Salem, and Boston were strongly influenced by Calvin, most were not true Presbyterians. They were, in fact, more like Congregationalists. Some of the earliest settlers in Massachusetts were Presbyterians, but the first real influx of Presbyterians to America was in the mid-1600s. In the early 1700s in New England, Jonathan Edwards triggered the Great

14. In the very early seventeenth century a Dutch Roman Catholic theologian, Cornelis Jansenius, proposed an extremely severe doctrine of predestination and the total depravity of man, discouraging frequent reception of Communion. Known as Jansenism, it was condemned as heresy. There are still a few practicing Jansenists in the Netherlands.

15. Today Geneva is still thought of as the "capital" of Protestantism. The World Council of Churches is headquartered there.

16. Politics were as much a part of the Westminster Assembly as was religion. In 1649 the Calvinists under Cromwell murdered Charles I, outlawed the Church of England, and held power under a dictatorship until the restoration of James II to the throne in 1660.

Awakening, which resulted in a missionary zeal leading to the spread of Presbyterianism throughout America. The church grew rapidly, becoming one of the major Protestant denominations. The first serious crisis came in 1861, shortly after South Carolina seceded from the Union and several other southern states followed suit. A split took place between the northern and southern portions of Presbyterianism, ultimately resulting in the northern "United Presbyterian Church" (UPC) and the "Presbyterian Church of the United States (Southern)" (PCUS). This schism was healed in 1983 with the formation of the "Presbyterian Church (U.S.A.)," commonly referred to as the PCUSA.[17] Presbyterians see this not as the creation of a new denomination, but as a reconciliation and reuniting of that which was split as a result of pre–Civil War tensions.

In 1973, prior to the PCUSA's formation, dissatisfaction grew in the PCUS (Southern) over liberal views regarding the deity of Jesus, biblical interpretation, and social values. A group of dissidents met in Birmingham, Alabama, and formed the conservative "Presbyterian Church in America" (PCA). In 1982 they were joined by the Reformed Presbyterian Church, making them the second largest Presbyterian group in America (the PCUSA is by far the largest). They have a strict traditional Calvinist orientation, affirming the doctrines of the total depravity of man and double predestination.

There are several other small Presbyterian groups in America, each emphasizing different aspects of traditional Presbyterian faith or practice. As in every other Protestant denomination there is always a flux of schisms and mergers, and there is always tension over one issue or another. There are a number of highly controversial issues being continually explored, including abortion and the ordination of homosexuals. These, of course, are sensitive issues in all denominations.

Presbyterianism, with about four and a half million members, is a significant force in American Protestantism. While not the largest of the Protestant denominations (that honor goes to the Baptists), it is certainly among the most respected.

17. This is not to be confused with PECUSA, which stands for the old name of the Episcopal Church ("Protestant Episcopal Church of the United States of America"). In 1976 the General Convention dropped the word "Protestant" from the title, so the Episcopal Church is now known as ECUSA.

THE BAPTISTS

The term "Baptist" refers to a movement rather than to a denomination or theological position. There is no Baptist denomination — the Baptists are made up of independent, autonomous congregations, with no set theology or administrative structure. The Baptists' common origins and traditions have led them to develop mutual support groups, which they call conventions or associations. These associations have no more authority than their member congregations choose to give them through their bylaws. In the United States there are 38 million Baptists in twenty-three major groups.[1] Their name refers to a practice that all Baptists have in common (though it is not exclusive to them) — namely, baptism only of professed believers, and only by total immersion. Despite their name, the group's main focus is not on baptism but on the regeneration and conversion of individuals. Membership in a Baptist church is open exclusively to those who can claim a personal experience of the Christian faith and life. The experience must be personal — simple assent to doctrine is not enough. Baptism is an outward sign of that experience, and is of-

1. These numbers are from the 1996 Yearbook of the National Council of Churches. They do not include 5 million who are members of Baptist offshoot groups such as the Disciples of Christ and the Churches of God. The largest groups are the Southern Baptist Convention (16 million), the National Baptist Convention, U.S.A. (8 million), the National Baptist Convention of America (3.5 million), the National Missionary Baptist Convention of America (2.5 million), and the Progressive National Baptist Convention (2.5 million).

140

ten seen as a token of spiritual rebirth — thus the expression "born again Christian."[2]

Baptists stress their divine origins, averring that they have no human founder, no human authority, and no human creed. Many claim a direct and unbroken succession from John the Baptist and the apostolic church. These individuals object to being called Protestant, since they deny being descendants of the Protestant Reformation.[3] Others claim descent from the Anabaptists,[4] a sixteenth-century Reformation group. Most scholars, however, trace the origins of the Baptist movement to seventeenth-century Puritanism, an offshoot of early Congregationalism.

History

In the early days of the movement, there were two distinct groups: the Particular Baptists and the General Baptists. The Particular Baptists had their roots in the English non-Separatist Calvinist movement.[5] They believed in a strict interpretation of Calvin's doctrine of particular atonement (predestination),[6] teaching that Christ died only for the elect — those chosen in advance for exclusive salvation. The General Baptists, rooted in the Puritan Separatist movement, believed that Christ died for all mankind, and that all who accepted him as their

2. This phrase, of course, refers to Jesus' statement to Nicodemus in John 3:3, "Except a man be born again, he cannot see the kingdom of God" (KJV).

3. In most English-speaking countries, the term "Protestant" is commonly used to mean "not Roman Catholic." Its correct use, however, denotes only the direct descendants of the European Protestant Reformation.

4. The Anabaptists denied the validity of infant baptism, requiring re-baptism of all who had been baptized as infants. Their name comes from the Greek for "baptize again." Their core beliefs were much like those of modern Baptists. For more information about the Anabaptists, see the chapter on the Mennonites.

5. The Separatists and the non-Separatists were both Congregationalists, believing adamantly in the separation of church and state. The Separatists believed that the Church of England was false, and had to be abolished (separated from the true Body of Christ). The non-Separatists simply wanted not to be part of it.

6. See the chapter on Presbyterianism for a more complete discussion of predestination and Arminianism.

Savior would be saved. This belief was closer to that of the Dutch reformer Jacobus Arminius.

The period of 1640-60 brought phenomenal growth. Huge numbers of Cromwell's Puritan soldiers were converted around the campfires during the British Civil War. The Particular Baptists made the most gains, while the General Baptists saw increasing defections to the Quakers and Unitarians. After the Restoration in 1660, religious persecution diminished the numbers but strengthened the resolve of the Baptists. By the time of the Act of Toleration in 1689, the General Baptists had all but disappeared and the Particular Baptists, although they had grown slowly during the persecutions, had retreated into a rigid and uncompromising Calvinism. The movement continued to grow during the following two centuries, and with the formation of missionary movements it was introduced to every corner of the British Empire. Today, the Baptist World Alliance represents millions of Baptists around the world, including huge and rapidly growing numbers in Asia, Africa, and the former Soviet Union.

In the American colonies, the first true Baptist Church was established in Providence, Rhode Island, in 1639 by Roger Williams after his banishment from Massachusetts. The movement spread and grew rapidly throughout America. Most Baptists were fervent supporters of the American Revolution, and thus the movement was looked upon warmly by many of the colonists. It did face legal difficulties in several places, however. In New England there was a church tax, whose revenue supported the Congregational Church. The Baptists, believing resolutely in the separation of church and state, were frequently jailed or had their churches closed for refusal to pay the tax. In Virginia, preachers were licensed, and many agents refused to license Baptists.[7]

The Baptist movement eventually became so large that distinct variations in worship and discipline became evident, particularly between the old established Northern churches and the newer Southern ones that had more recently made inroads into the firmly established Anglican, Presbyterian, and Methodist regions. Most of the Southern Baptist churches were the result of a renewed religious fervor that

7. One such preacher was John Leland, a close friend of Thomas Jefferson. He threatened to run against Jefferson for a seat in the Virginia General Assembly until Jefferson promised to work for legislation supporting the separation of church and state.

came from the revivalist activities of the Methodists and the Great Awakening. The North adhered strongly to the "old ways," while the Southern churches were much more involved in the enthusiasm of revivals and camp-meetings — what the North called "emotional excesses" and "ecclesiastical irregularities."

While these differences surfaced and were healed many times, one issue between North and South arose that was to become critical. That, of course, was slavery. After several failed attempts to reach a compromise, the Southern Baptist Convention was organized in 1845 at Augusta, Georgia. While it was framed on essentially the same structure as its parent convention, it endorsed slavery. It devoted almost all of its missionary efforts to foreign missions. The Northern home missions therefore continued in the South until the start of the war in 1860, and resumed in 1865. As the South recovered, the Southern Baptists began their own home missions in an attempt to push out what they saw as Northern interference. The rift was rendered permanent in 1907 with the formation of the Northern Baptist Convention.[8] This brought together most of the existing Baptist groups in the North, and accepted a regionally allocated territorial authority between the North and the South.

The Northern Baptists were never officially racially segregated, though *de facto* segregation existed from the beginning. The Southern Baptist Convention was officially segregated until after the passage of the 1964 Civil Rights Act. A large majority of Southern Baptist churches are still segregated by circumstance or by choice. Most of the black churches appear to be at least as content with this situation as the white ones. Baptist teachings had a strong appeal to slaves and free blacks alike, and black churches were an integral part of the movement from its earliest days in America. The black National Baptist Convention was organized in 1880. By 1900 black Baptists outnumbered the total of all other black Christians, and today over 85 percent of American blacks are Baptist. Most of America's leading black social activists — including Martin Luther King Jr., Al Sharpton, and Jesse Jackson — have been Baptist ministers.

The twentieth century saw a series of schisms in the Baptist move-

8. In 1950 this was renamed the American Baptist Convention, and in 1972 it changed again to the American Baptist Churches in the United States of America (ABCUSA).

ment. By 1900 the old rigid Calvinism had all but disappeared and had been replaced with a strongly evangelistic attitude known as "evangelicalism." This appealed to emotion and "heart religion" and was open to the new ultra-liberal "modernist" movement that threatened (and was resisted by) all the major Christian denominations including a large portion of the Baptists of the time. A strong Baptist proponent of modernism was the renowned preacher Harry Emerson Fosdick. A counter-reaction to modernism called "fundamentalism" arose, espousing an effort to restore the fundamental teachings of the apostolic church.[9] This led to many controversies and the formation of a number of smaller Baptist conventions. The final result of this, however, was that outside the South there developed a distaste for theology among the majority of Baptists. They became increasingly nontheological, expressing their unity by turning their attention to religious activities and personal spirituality. Recently, however, many Baptist leaders have begun recognizing the need for a renewal of theological inquiry. The Southern Baptists have been torn on this issue. Some have accepted a more liberal interpretation of their traditional teachings, while others have fought modernism by applying a strict literal interpretation of Scripture to all aspects of their spiritual, moral, and social lives. Recently this has led to an ongoing power struggle between moderate and conservative groups in the Southern Baptist Convention. Many leaders see these struggles as productive, forcing a deeper examination of the issues.

Beliefs and Practices

There are six basic beliefs that unite all Baptists, despite their differences. While they avoid formal doctrinal definition of them, these core beliefs are the heart of the Baptist movement:

(1) The Bible is the supreme authority in all matters of faith or practice. Creeds or doctrinal statements are only for explanation or enlightenment, but never for the promulgation of doctrine.

---

9. Most (but not all) fundamentalists are also literalists. Literalists believe in a literal interpretation of the Bible, and the term "fundamentalism" has now become synonymous with literalism.

(2) Baptism is for believers only. It has no sacramental authority, but is the initiatory rite signifying the believer's public profession of faith and acknowledgment of a personal relationship with Christ. For this reason it is administered only to committed believers. Following John the Baptist's practice, it is administered only by total immersion.[10]

(3) The church is made up exclusively of believers. Each congregation is an autonomous assembly of those who, in order to be accepted as members, must give firm evidence of their commitment to Christ and of their living a holy life.

(4) All Christians are equal in the eyes of the church. There is no rank or privilege, and by the doctrine of the priesthood of all believers every Christian is a minister to all other Christians. While pastors are elected by the local church to serve them and preach, they bear no sacramental or priestly status and are recognized simply as equals who are specially trained for a specific role.

(5) The local congregation is independent and autonomous. A duly constituted congregation is fully capable of ministering to its own members, with no outside help other than from God. This is not to imply detachment from other churches, however. In keeping with the priesthood of all believers, each congregation has an obligation to minister to other congregations. Thus associations and conventions are formed for mutual aid and support, and to testify to unity in Christ. They have no formal administrative authority, however.

(6) The church and the state must be separate. This has been a basic doctrine since the beginning of the movement in England. Baptists were primarily responsible for urging Congress to put the religious freedom clauses in the Constitution and the First Amendment.[11] Only Christ — no human, and no civil power — can have authority over the church.

---

10. The majority of Christians accept baptism by two other methods as well. These are aspersion (sprinkling) and affusion (pouring of water on the head). Most, including the Baptists, require that water be used and the name of the Holy Trinity invoked (Matt. 28:19).

11. In a letter to the Danbury (Connecticut) Baptist Association, in response to their plea to repeal the church tax, President Thomas Jefferson, a Deist, coined the phrase "a wall of separation between church and state." His unquestioned intent, as is evidenced in many of his writings, was to protect the church from the state, not vice versa.

In many Baptists' minds there is question as to whether non-Baptists should be considered truly Christian. Most are not so sectarian, however, as to make an issue of this. In fact, most Baptist associations have been active in ecumenical and certain interdenominational activities, including the National and World Councils of Churches, in the hope that their example might serve to inspire others to repentance and conversion.

For most of the history of the movement the pastor was thought of as the leader of the local congregation; although equal to all the members, he was considered the first among equals. His deacons were his assistants and agents, and he presided over the congregation. In recent times the pastor has come to be seen more as an employee of the congregation, while the boards of deacons have expanded and are looked upon as an authority figure. A lay moderator is the executive officer. Traditionally important decisions are made by democratic vote of the congregation, but of late there has been a tendency, particularly in the North, to turn much of the decision-making over to the board of deacons. This narrowing of authority is inconsistent with the Congregationalist roots of the Baptist movement, but only time will tell where it will ultimately lead.

Worship

Baptist worship is very similar to that of the early Congregational Puritans. It is centered on preaching, particularly the exposition of Scripture. Extemporaneous prayer is preferred to the use of prescribed prayers, and hymns and musical selections are a major part of worship. Each congregation determines its own form of worship, but most follow these patterns. Hymnals and service outlines are furnished by the convention, but these are simply offered as aids to the local clergy and laity in developing their services. There is no set or required form of worship. Most congregations celebrate the "Lord's Supper" (Communion) quarterly, although some do so monthly and a very few weekly. (If weekly Communion takes place, it would usually be in churches which have two Sunday services, one of which would be a Communion service.) Baptists do not see Communion as sacramental, but as a memorial of the Last Supper and a symbol of

Christ's saving sacrifice. Likewise, as we saw, baptism was not considered a sacrament, but an initiatory rite denoting the believer's public avowal that he commits himself to Christ, willingly and knowingly receives Christ's spiritual cleansing, and accepts Christ as a personal Savior.

THE QUAKERS

The Quakers are a nonstructured, nonliturgical, intensely peace-loving group that relies for all its thinking and action on the guidance of the Holy Spirit. Their proper name is "The Society of Friends," although they were originally known as "Children of Truth" and "Children of Light." Today they generally call themselves simply "Friends" or "Quakers," a term that was originally pejorative. No Quaker takes offense at the term today — in fact, most use it. The early Friends, like many other Spirit-centered groups, often trembled, shook, or rocked while praying. It is believed that outsiders derisively called them "Quakers" because of this behavior. George Fox, their founder, disarmed this insult by adopting the name. He wrote in 1650, "Justice Bennet of Derby first called us Quakers because we bid them tremble at the word of God."

Worship and Beliefs

The basic tenets of the Quaker movement are simple, although they developed over a period of time. Quakers believe in the "inward light," the awareness of a personal relationship with God through the guidance of the Holy Spirit. Their worship is open to anyone who wishes to attend and usually involves silently waiting for personal inspiration. Anyone is free to speak if he feels moved by God to do so. It is not rare that they will gather together, remain in silence for a long period, pray silently, and go home. They do not embrace formal systems or disciplines of meditation, but simply try to clear their minds and open them to the presence of the Holy Spirit. There are no sacraments, and no rites for marriage or burial. Marriage is confirmed simply by the declaration of the couple and the approval of the congregation, and burial is performed by gathering at the graveside and silently contemplating the presence of God. There is no baptism — one becomes a member by affirming his desire to do so, testifying to his faith, and receiving the approval of the congregation.

Quakers reject the term "Trinity" as unscriptural, but they affirm the Godhead of the Father, the Son, and the Holy Spirit. They believe in the Atonement by Christ's death and resurrection, and in the guidance of the Holy Spirit. There is little attention paid to traditional ecclesiastical celebrations such as Christmas and Easter; these are considered man-made feasts since they were not observed as festal celebrations in the Bible. Quakers also reject formal creeds as man-made, although their teachings are in full accord with the basic tenets of the Apostles' Creed. They do not refer to their places of worship as churches but as "meeting-houses." George Fox, the founder of the Quaker faith, repudiated what he called "steeple-houses," and while he recognized that as congregations grew they needed more than just homes for meetings, he expected the meeting-houses to be as simple and plain as possible. They were to be nothing more than convenient gathering places.

In America, most congregations, in addition to worshiping at least weekly, have a monthly meeting in which they deal with any business that needs to come before them. In England such meetings usually involve a number of congregations who meet together. There are also often regional quarterly and annual meetings. Any Friend may attend — there are no elected or appointed delegates — and the only official is a clerk. He does not preside in the parliamentary sense, but simply moderates so as to "gather the sense of the meeting." Quakers have no ordained clergy, but there are "recorded ministers" or "public friends" who are free to "travel in the ministry," teaching and counseling. These are men and women whose lives are obviously righteous and whose personal testimony witnesses to a deep faith. In their own congregations they are usually leaders in the good works of the congregation, such as ministry to the suffering and needy. It is important to

Quakers, however, that these ministers be considered to have no more authority than any other worshiper.

Quakers avoid worldly values, especially actions or attitudes that could damage another person. For this reason they are pacifists, refusing to engage in any physical conflict, from warfare to a common fist-fight. Likewise, they will not declare bankruptcy, considering this to be equivalent to stealing from their creditors. When William Penn went bankrupt, he struggled for years to pay off all his debts in full. Quakers will not swear oaths. They maintain that an oath is an offense to God because a godly man is as good as his word, and taking an oath implies a lack of trustworthiness. In slave days, any traffic in slavery or ownership of slaves that was not repented for was a very serious offense. Even so, they considered activities such as the "underground railroad" to be equivalent to theft. Until well into the nineteenth century, marriage "out of meeting" (marriage with a non-Quaker) was forbidden. They will not acknowledge worldly titles or customs such as bowing or tipping the hat, as these are considered signs of vanity. For example, they will show full respect to a judge, but most will not address him as "Your Honor." They also believe strongly in the total separation of church and state, and in past times when church taxes existed in many states, they forbade the payment of them. Violation of any of these principles could incur discipline, the most severe punishment being "disownment." (Disownment is still technically held as a discipline, but it is very rarely used today.) To be disowned meant to be unwelcome to participate in any community activity, social or spiritual. It was not quite as severe as the early Anabaptist "ban," but it must have been a terrible thing to a rural Quaker whose religious community was his sole social contact.

One basic and important principle of the Quakers is their sense of responsibility to mankind. From the earliest days their relief work has been extensive. This is partly a result of their own suffering during the times of persecution. Instead of making them vengeful, it sensitized them to the suffering of others. Their programs have been so extensive that when the American Friends Service Committee received the Nobel Peace Prize in 1947, many newspapers identified the Quakers as a philanthropic organization rather than a religious one. Quaker teaching, though, is that if the Atonement was an act of the love of God, then we have a moral duty to reflect that love to all mankind. Until the

nineteenth century the Quakers, while they generously assisted anyone in distress, rarely involved themselves in social activism. Their
first great social reform activity was women's suffrage — most of the
early suffragist leaders were Quakers. Today Quakers are very active
in everything from civil rights work to human rights movements such
as Amnesty International. Many Quakers have been involved in public service, including two presidents, Hoover and Nixon.

History

During the period of the English Revolution there were many groups
that had given up on expecting any spiritual guidance from the active
churches of the time — Roman, Anglican, or any of the Protestant bodies. Their search was satisfied by a flood of speakers, mainly from the
north, who called upon them to seek a direct contact with God. The
most prominent of these was George Fox (1624-91). He was the son of
a wealthy weaver, and was raised in the Church of England. His parents encouraged him to become a priest, but he rebelled against what
he called the "hireling ministry." After a long spiritual struggle he developed a theology of his own, based solely on the Bible. He proposed
the concept of the "inner light," and in 1647 he began to preach his
concept of spirituality. The movement caught on very quickly. Within
the first ten years there were over sixty thousand converts from all social classes (the least by far came from the two social extremes, the aristocracy and the laboring class). They were spread all over the British
Isles, although the greatest concentration was in the north around
Lancashire and Yorkshire, and the least in Scotland and Wales. Many
migrated to America, but for the most part they were not well received
there.

The Roman and Anglican clergy tended to ignore the Quakers as
just another misguided Protestant insurgence, but the Puritans faced
them with nothing less than rage, both in England and in America.
While the Puritans encouraged a personal relationship with God, they
felt that the Quakers' idea of this was insolent and intolerably familiar.
By 1660, however, the Friends had offended the Anglicans and Romans to the extent that they, too, persecuted them. When Charles II
was restored to the throne, the only change was that the Puritans also

were on the receiving end of the persecution. Even so, rather than becoming brothers in suffering, they went out of their way to make life miserable for the Quakers. Among the Quaker principles that were most offensive to the establishment were a refusal to swear oaths, serve in the military, and pay "tithes" (taxes to support the established church). Over fifteen thousand Quakers were imprisoned, and while none were executed, hundreds died because of the wretched prison conditions. Nevertheless, the movement continued to grow.

As the number of Quakers in America increased, in 1656 a group of women preachers began actively proselytizing in the Maryland and Massachusetts Bay Colonies. They were cruelly persecuted and in Boston four were put to death, but even so the movement grew. Soon the majority of Rhode Island's population was Quaker, and Quakers were found in ever increasing numbers throughout the colonies.

By far the largest number of Quakers was in Pennsylvania. In 1681 Charles II granted William Penn a charter to establish a Quaker colony. Penn envisioned it as a "holy experiment," testing whether a government based on Quaker principles of pacifism and religious toleration could succeed. Charles, of course, simply saw it as a convenient way to get rid of the Quakers in England. The "experiment" courted disaster. Its religious tolerance allowed for a majority of hostile non-Quakers to settle there, and in the midst of a violent society on a wild and untamed continent, its pacifism disallowed any attempt at self-defense. On top of that, Penn was so entangled in affairs at home that he spent more time in England than in Pennsylvania. He showed poor judgment in selecting the deputies he sent there in his place, many of whom were non-Quakers and were frequently at odds with the Quaker-dominated legislature. He was also a poor manager of money and finally went bankrupt. Even so, the Quaker principles held sway in Pennsylvania until 1756, when the French and Indian War required that they fight or die. At that point the system began to break down, and soon the non-Quakers dominated the legislature. Voltaire observed that Penn's treaties with the Indians were the only ones never sworn to and never violated. This was not quite true, but Pennsylvania's relationship with the Indians was better than that of any other colony or territory. Pennsylvania became completely involved in the American Revolution — it was, after all, the home of Philadelphia, the first American capital, and of Valley Forge, one of the first major

152

American military bases. Even so, the Pennsylvanian Quakers would not fight on either side.

By the end of the eighteenth century, more by evolution than by intent, the Quakers had developed an identifiable dress and language — very plain, old-fashioned clothing, and a corrupted version of Jacobean ("Bible") language.[1] This lasted into the twentieth century, and was valued because it gave them a unique identity and reminded them of their moral obligations. Most Quakers today use contemporary language and dress in modern but simple clothing. The eighteenth- and nineteenth-century Quakers were for the most part farmers and workmen, although there were many who were cultured, well-educated, and in leadership positions in government and society. They were rigid in their family discipline. Children could marry only with the permission of their parents, and violation of this could be punished with being "disowned." Most Quakers were the children of Quakers, and less and less attention was paid to making converts. They were adamantly opposed to slavery, and by 1800 all Friends had emancipated their own slaves. English Quakers worked actively for abolition of slavery in the British Empire. American Quakers, on the other hand, while they were intolerant of any Quaker owning a slave, did little toward the abolition of the institution.[2]

The rise of the evangelical movement and the influence of Wesley's teachings gradually moved the Quakers into a closer cooperation with other Christian churches, and a body of evangelical Friends arose in England. Until then there had been little concern with theology among Quakers. Although they did not deny the majority of the traditional Protestant doctrines, their primary focus had been the "inward light." While not out of favor with the traditional Quakers, the evangelical Friends became much more interested in promulgating the doctrines of the inerrancy and authority of the Bible and of the incarnation and Atonement of Christ. This evangelicalism was much slower to develop in America. Many Quakers were moving westward, and they associ-

---

1. The so-called "thees and thous" of Jacobean language degenerated into "thee" instead of the singular "you," regardless of grammatical case. While the Bible would say "Thou knowest whither thou goest," a Quaker would say, "Thee knows where thee are going."

2. Stephen Hopkins, a Quaker who was Governor of Rhode Island nine times, was disowned because he would not free his one slave.

ated the Philadelphia Quaker leaders with the rich upper classes. Many Quaker congregations were moving away from the traditional simple worship. This originally had consisted of simply sitting in silence; if someone felt moved by the Spirit to say something he would speak briefly, and then the group would return to silence. In the nineteenth century, especially in the western congregations, worship began to look more like traditional Protestant worship, with singing, Bible readings, oral prayers, and only brief periods of silence. Many congregations even called themselves "Quaker churches." In some there were paid ministers who preached sermons. Some had baptism and marriage ceremonies, and came to look much like Congregational churches. These innovations did not appear in England, although even there the traditional authority of parents and congregational elders had abated.

As in any major movement, there have been disagreements throughout the history of the Friends, although, true to their name, most have been resolved in a peaceful manner, or have resulted in separations with a minimum of rancor. One of the most significant schisms was that of a small group of radical eighteenth-century Quakers who adopted the French Camisards'[3] practice of shouting, speaking in tongues, running, whirling, shaking, and dancing as part of their worship. (A couple of centuries later these practices would have been called "pentecostal"). They called themselves the United Society of Believers in Christ's Second Coming, but because of their mode of worship they came to be called "The Shaking Quakers." This soon became simply "Shakers."[4] In 1758 Ann Lee, an illiterate mill worker in Manchester, England, was converted to this group. Soon thereafter "Mother Ann" had a series of revelations. She claimed to be the female aspect of God's dual nature, and a second incarnation of Christ, and

---

3. The Camisards were a small but strong sect of Huguenots who rose up against King Louis XIV in 1702. They instituted a brutal guerilla war in which they burned Roman Catholic churches and murdered their priests. In retribution Pope Clement XI issued a bull condemning them to death, and over 450 Huguenot villages were slaughtered and burned. The rebellion finally died out in 1710. The name "Camisards" referred to the black smocks that were their uniform. Their worship was excited, emotional, and physically active, and was scorned by the mainstream Huguenots.

4. This name, like "Quakers," was originally used as an insult, but was quickly adopted and used by the United Society of Believers.

her followers accepted her as such. She established celibacy as the primary principle of righteousness, and required this of all her followers. She and eight of her followers, obeying a vision, came to America in 1774. They established a community in upstate New York and began to grow rapidly. In the following decades it grew at an astonishing rate, especially considering that as a celibate sect, growth could only happen by conversion. By the 1840s there were Shaker villages spread from Maine to Kentucky, with over six thousand members. After the Civil War the group began to decline, and today there is only one active village left, although several still survive as museums. In 1965 the remaining Shakers decided to accept no new conversions, and let the sect die. Sabbath Day Lake, Maine, is the only surviving active Shaker village, with only a handful of members living on a small corner of the property. Shaker life is simple, and the utilitarian austerity of their furniture has become an honored American art form. When the last Shakers die, no new furniture made in the traditional style will be considered truly Shaker. This has made the existing pieces coveted and very expensive, in direct contrast to the Quaker and Shaker principles of simplicity.

The spiritual freedom of the Society of Friends makes it very attractive to many Christians but is also a significant impediment to its being brought back into a reunited church. A reunited church would have, by its very nature, established teachings, rites, and ceremonies, and this is antithetical to the basic concept of the Quaker faith. The free faith of the Quakers was well described by Albert Schweitzer in *The Quest for the Historical Jesus*, when he wrote that "as we do the work of Christ we shall come to know who he is."

THE METHODISTS

The twentieth century was one of reunion in the Methodist Church, healing a series of rifts that occurred in the previous centuries. In 1939 the Methodist Episcopal Church,[1] the Methodist Episcopal Church South, and the Methodist Protestant Church merged, calling the new united body the Methodist Church. In 1968 this merged with the Evangelical United Brethren to form the present United Methodist Church (UMC), by far the largest of the Methodist bodies.[2] This is the group we usually think of when we use the term "Methodist."

History

The first roots of Methodism were at Oxford University, where a group of students, led by the brothers John (1703-91) and Charles

1. The term "Episcopal" in their title has nothing to do with the Episcopal Church. It refers to the fact that the Methodist church is administered by bishops. Unlike Anglican (Episcopal) bishops, however, they are not in the historic or apostolic succession. They have administrative authority, but are not considered a separate order of sacramentally ordained clergy.

2. According to the 1995 National Council of Churches census, the major Methodist groups in the United States, in order of size, are the United Methodist, African Methodist Episcopal, African Methodist Episcopal Zion, Wesleyan, Free Methodist, Evangelical Methodist, Southern Methodist, Primitive Methodist, Allegheny Wesleyan Methodist Connection, and Fundamental Methodist churches.

(1707-88) Wesley, developed a disciplined and systematic program of prayer and Bible reading. They called their program "the method." They were ridiculed by other students as the "Bible Bigots" and the "Methodists," and this latter name stuck.[3] They endured the derision, however, and diligently preached and ministered to poor and uneducated people in England. At this time the Church of England had slipped into a period of self-satisfaction and latitudinarianism, appealing to the slovenly theology and undisciplined morals (or lack thereof) of the upper classes. The Methodists hoped to reawaken the church to its mission. It would not be until many years later that they would break away from the Church of England and reform themselves as a Protestant denomination.

John and Charles Wesley were the fifteenth and eighteenth sons of Samuel Wesley, an Anglican priest. They, like their father, were firmly loyal to the teachings and traditions of the Church of England, despite the laxity into which the church had fallen. After graduating from Oxford they were ordained to the priesthood and assigned to the Georgia colony — John as a missionary, and Charles as secretary to Governor Oglethorpe. They arrived in 1735. Their mission was less than successful, and they returned to England, Charles in 1736, and John early in 1738. They never again went to America, although they kept close contact with the American movement. In May of 1738 both men independently had major religious experiences that fired in them a zeal to revive the Church of England. The challenge they faced is exemplified by the story (probably apocryphal) that when John Wesley told the bishop of London that the church needed a rebirth of zeal and enthusiasm, the bishop coolly replied, "Mr. Wesley, zeal and enthusiasm are vulgar emotions."

Despite the lackluster attitude of the Church of England, the Wesleys worked diligently and inspired a continually growing following. Many of their disciples carried their mission to the American colonies. American Methodism began as a lay movement, with most of its important leaders, both men and women, rising from the ranks of the

---

3. In the same way the early Christians, who called their belief "The Way," were ridiculed as *Crestianes* ("followers of the Fool"). At some point this became *Christianes* ("followers of the Messiah"), and the name "Christian" stuck. It was in Antioch that they were first called Christians (Acts 11:26). Similarly, "Lutheran" and "Quaker" were originally used as pejoratives.

common people — farmers, shopkeepers, and craftsmen. In 1769-71 John Wesley sent trained lay preachers to America to help organize the rapidly growing movement. One of these was Francis Asbury, whose devotion, enthusiasm, and ability made him the most important figure in early American Methodism. He effectively shaped the denomination into the form it still bears today.

John Wesley had instituted a system of regular conferences of Methodist leaders in England in order to strengthen and oversee the activities of the movement. In 1773 a conference of the top ten Methodist leaders was held in Philadelphia to define the goals and organize the structure of the American movement. Among other important actions, they affirmed their loyalty to the principles taught by John Wesley and to those of the Church of England. They also vowed that since they were laymen, they would not presume to administer the sacraments. Like many Anglicans of the time, they only acknowledged the sacraments of baptism and Communion to have any real significance. They acknowledged the necessity of the sacraments, stating that their followers should receive them at their local Anglican parish church. They placed a strong emphasis on the self-discipline of preachers, individual worshipers, and congregations, and they set up a system of regular conferences similar to those established by Wesley.

Wesley made no effort to hide his loyalty to the crown and his strong opposition to the American Revolution. Likewise, a great many American Methodists were Tories and refused to support the rebellion, which seriously hurt the movement during the war. After America earned its independence, Wesley realized that it would be necessary to reduce the strong relationship that existed between British and American Methodists and to let the American branch develop more independently. In 1784 he sent Thomas Coke to oversee the work of Francis Asbury. Coke brought with him *The Sunday Service of the Methodists in North America,* a prayer book prepared by Wesley that incorporated his revision of the Church of England's Thirty-Nine Articles. Coke was accompanied by two lay preachers whom Wesley had ordained. These were not priests — he made no claim to have the authority to ordain priests — but were laymen whom he had trained and who he felt were qualified to preach the gospel. He had similarly ordained Thomas Coke a "bishop," not as a member of an ecclesiastical order in the apostolic succession, but simply as an administrator. It was an unfortunate use of terminology, however. This highly controversial act of ordaining angered many of the Anglican ecclesiastics of the time. In reality, it was roughly equivalent to today's practice in the Episcopal Church of licensing qualified lay readers to preach sermons of their own composition. Nevertheless, the very concept of a priest ordaining was foreign to Anglican thinking,[4] and it set a precedent that eventually contributed to the independence of the Methodist Church in America.

In 1784, the year that Coke arrived in America, the "Christmas Conference" was held in Baltimore. It was attended by almost all the Methodist lay preachers, including two emancipated slaves, one of whom was Richard Allen. He would later break from this group and found an independent Methodist Church. At this meeting they organized the movement as The Methodist Episcopal Church in America. This event can probably be considered the beginning of the Methodist Church as an independent American Protestant denomination. Even though the Methodists had been drifting further and further from Anglicanism over the years, until this time they had still considered themselves a movement within the Anglican Church.[5] In the years following they published the first *Methodist Book of Discipline* (1785), established quadrennial general conferences (the first in 1792), prepared a Constitution (1808), and established a publishing house. They became ardently involved in home missions and evangelism, mainly through revivals and camp meetings. They also built several schools, including Cokesbury College in Abingdon, Maryland, in 1787.[6]

During the next half century Methodism grew rapidly throughout America. Serious self-discipline and commitment were expected of all members. Wesley had condemned what he called "almost Christians," and the young church had no tolerance for such people. During this time there were other groups who were dedicated to the teachings of Wesley, many of whom would ultimately merge with the Methodists.

---

4. In Anglicanism only a bishop may ordain priests and deacons or license lay preachers.

5. It was this same year (1784) that another group of Anglicans, refusing to swear allegiance to King George III as the head of the church, sent Samuel Seabury to Scotland to be consecrated the first bishop of the Episcopal Church.

6. The college took its name from a combination of the names of Coke and Asbury. The Methodist publishing house, Abingdon-Cokesbury, in turn took its name from the college (it is now simply known as Cokesbury).

The Methodists were the chief proponents of the Sunday school movement, which had been brought to America by Francis Asbury in 1786, and they built the first American religious publishing house, the Methodist Book Concern. They devoted considerable resources to the development of Sunday schools and the publication of materials for them. This was a major source of conversions to Methodism.[7]

This period of growth also saw its share of challenges and crises. In 1816 Richard Allen, who believed he had been mistreated because of his race, withdrew and founded the African Methodist Episcopal Church. In 1821 another group of dissatisfied blacks formed the African Methodist Episcopal Zion Church. Because of the racial attitudes of the American culture of the time, blacks had worshiped separately from whites from the beginning, even though they had been considered part of the same movement until their schism. Another dissenting group demanded that the laity have voice, vote, and the authority to elect district superintendents. That group split off as well, calling itself the Methodist Protestant Church.

The advent of the Civil War caused the greatest split in the church. Wesley was adamantly opposed to slavery, an explosive issue in antebellum America. It came to a head when a Southern bishop, James Andrew, inherited five slaves. Local law prohibited his freeing them (which he was apparently not anxious to do, anyway). The 1844 general conference addressed the slavery issue for the first time and suspended Bishop Andrew for as long as he owned slaves. The Southern delegates immediately drew up a Plan of Separation, and in 1845 withdrew to form the Methodist Episcopal Church, South. Acrimony between the two bodies increased greatly in the ensuing years, although both churches flourished independently. The war devastated the Southern church — most of its properties were laid waste, its leadership was all but wiped out as battle casualties, and its morale destroyed. In spite of this, it rebuilt and multiplied fourfold by the end of the century. After the war the black membership of the Southern

---

7. The Sunday school movement was begun in England in 1780 by Robert Raikes, who originated it as a literacy program for London's street urchins. He believed that their lot would be greatly improved if they were able to read the Bible and memorize Bible passages. The program rapidly extended to illiterate adults, and then grew to a popular religious education program throughout the Church of England.

160

church withdrew to form the Colored Methodist Episcopal Church (now called the Christian Methodist Episcopal Church). During this period the Northern branch of the church, which had not been seriously damaged by the war, grew at an astonishing rate, enjoyed great prosperity, and became a major influence in American Protestantism. Both churches were very active in foreign missions as well as in evangelizing American Indians and freed slaves.

Two major issues with which both groups struggled for decades were the role of the laity and that of women. It was not until the early twentieth century that the laity were granted full representative rights in the general conference, and women were not admitted to the clergy until 1939 in the Northern or Southern churches.

Finally in the middle years of the twentieth century all the Methodist bodies developed an intense interest in ecumenism and a restoration of unity, and the mergers mentioned earlier occurred, creating the United Methodist Church, which has a present membership of just under 9 million. (The next largest membership is that of the two African Methodist Episcopal groups, which include 4.5 million Methodists.[8])

Organization

At the local church level, authority rests in the minister and a board of laymen elected by the congregation. They are responsible for the worship, physical facilities, and finances of the local church. A district is made up of a group of local churches, and is headed by a clergyman called the district superintendent. The districts make up the annual conference, which is governed by a bishop. The bishop is named for life, but he is not seen as a separate order from the rest of the clergy as he is in the polity of the Catholic churches. The episcopate in the Methodist church is more administrative than sacramental. There is a quadrennial general conference, which is the top unit of ecclesiastical government on the national level. It is equivalent to the Episcopal Church's general convention. Methodist government is a tripartite system of checks and balances, much like the United States govern-

---

8. The African Methodist Episcopal (A.M.E.) Church is an American church made up almost exclusively of African-Americans.

ment — the general conference is legislative, disputes are settled by the nine-member judicial court, and the council of bishops is the executive branch.

Beliefs and Customs

Methodists believe that the Bible is the primary source of all Christian doctrine. While tradition is valued as the continuing story of the activity of Christ in the world, it is not considered a valid source of doctrine. Reason is also greatly valued as a gift of God by which Scripture can be interpreted and doctrine discerned. Grace is a pivotal doctrine in Methodism. It is the unmerited and loving intervention of God in human experience, transmitted through the Holy Spirit. Methodists emphasize three aspects of God's grace: prevenient grace, which precedes salvation and guides us to the Christian life; justifying grace, which enables us to accept salvation and the gifts of the Holy Spirit; and sanctifying grace, which is the fulfillment of salvation and elevates us to perfect union with Christ.

Like most Protestants, Methodists believe that we are justified solely by faith, and not by good works. They accept good works as a sign of the presence of faith, but not as a source of faith or justification. Catholics believe that while good works are the fruit of faith and are not sufficient by themselves to gain justification, they also are a means of strengthening and developing faith, and thus can lead to justification.

Methodists accept only baptism and Communion as sacraments. In the past decade there has been a distinct shift to a stronger emphasis on the sacraments in the spirituality and worship of Methodism. In 1988 the general conference instituted an in-depth study of the theology and significance of baptism, and in 1996 a similar study was begun to examine and refine the Eucharistic theology of the church.

Methodists believe that baptism initiates us into the church, the body of Christ. Since this is a pure gift of grace and not something we can merit, then individual personal commitment is not a necessary prerequisite. For this reason Methodists encourage the baptism of infants. They honor the baptism of all Christian denominations, believing that Christ instituted baptism as a sacrament of unity rather than of divisiveness. They see it as a spiritual washing away of human sinfulness, and they accept the doctrine of original sin, which teaches that humans have as a part of their fallen nature the tendency to sin. Baptism removes from us the responsibility for this flaw, leaving us responsible thereafter only for the actual sins that we commit.

Methodists believe that Christ is spiritually present in Holy Communion through the faith of the recipients of the sacrament. To Methodists the Eucharist is a sacred meal in which the church proclaims God's grace and reenacts the Last Supper as a symbol of Christ's spiritual feeding of the faithful. For many years they have rejected the Catholic doctrine that Christ's glorified Body and Blood are objectively present in the elements of bread and wine (the "real presence"). Today, however, more and more Methodists are returning to an acceptance of the real presence, which was Wesley's belief. Modern Methodist interpretations of the Sacrament thus range from seeing it as pure symbolism to a belief in Christ's objective presence.

The summary of the faith accepted by Methodists is expressed in the Nicene and Apostles' Creeds. These teachings, along with those of the Bible, of course, form the backbone of Methodist theology. There is no tightly defined structure of dogmatic theology in Methodism; the teachings are based on those of John Wesley, which are rooted in the thinking of both the Anglican and Protestant reformers. Methodism did not arise as the result of a theological dispute, but as a movement seeking a deeper spirituality and social responsibility than was to be found in the organized churches of the time. To this day the emphasis in Methodism is not on specific theological or liturgical issues, but on the development of a strong personal relationship with Christ through self-discipline and social conscience.

THE "CHRISTIANS"

The Disciples of Christ and the Churches of Christ

There are three groups in the movement known as the "Christian churches," which was founded by the preachers Barton W. Stone and Thomas and Alexander Campbell. Today the original group, now known as the Christian Church (Disciples of Christ), still often refers to itself by its early name, the Stone-Campbell Movement. From this group grew the Churches of Christ, who withdrew because of disputes over the authority and interpretation of Scripture. A third group appeared in 1968, the Undenominational Fellowship of Christian Churches and Churches of Christ. They disagreed with the Disciples of Christ about organizational structure and ecumenical activities.

History

Although he lived most of his life in the United States, Alexander Campbell was born in 1788 in the north part of Ireland, of well-educated and pious Presbyterian parents. His father, Thomas, was of Scottish descent, and his mother was of French Huguenot origin. Thomas served as a pastor and educator in Ireland, but he had a deep-seated desire to "unite all Christians in one communion on a purely Scriptural basis." The irony, of course, is that such dreams almost inevitably end in fragmenting the church even more. Sometime in the first decade of the nineteenth century Thomas left for America to pursue this dream, having made plans for his family to join him after he got settled. In 1808 Alexander set off for America, but he was shipwrecked on the Scottish coast. He took this opportunity to enroll at the University of Glasgow and begin preparation for the Presbyterian ministry. In 1809 he went to America, and joined his father in Washington County, Pennsylvania. There his father had founded the "Christian Association of Washington." Its stated purpose was

> to establish no new sect, but to persuade Christians to abandon party names and creeds, sectarian usages and denominational strife, and associate in Christian fellowship, in the common faith in a divine Lord, with no other terms of religious communion than faith in and obedience to the Lord Jesus Christ.

Alexander, building on the principles set forth by his father, officially organized the movement at Brush Run, Pennsylvania, and on January 1, 1812, he was ordained a minister. His zeal is unquestioned — in the first year he preached 106 sermons — but his inflexibility cost him any hope of real success. As he interpreted the Bible he could find no justification for infant baptism, and required baptism by immersion only. By so doing he cut off the vast majority of Christians in the region, most of whom were of Methodist, Lutheran, and Reformed backgrounds, all of which accept infant baptism. In the summer of 1812 he, along with his wife and his parents, was re-baptized by immersion. He tried to unite with the local Baptists, but only on the condition that he would be free to preach his own interpretation of what he read in the Bible. The Baptists did not take well to this, and while they cooperated to some extent, they did not support him strongly. He called his followers "Disciples of Christ," but they were popularly called "Christians" or "Campbellites." They were dedicated to observing only the practices that were recorded in the Bible. They repudiated all "speculative theology" and "emotional revivalism," and maintained a puritanical simplicity in their worship.

The movement grew very slowly — by 1817 there were only 150 members. In 1832 his followers joined with the so-called "Christian Church" of the Kentucky preacher Barton W. Stone. Stone, like Campbell, had been raised a Presbyterian, and he shared with the Campbells the dream of a unified Christianity. The teachings of both were essentially the same, and the united group usually referred to itself as the

"Stone-Campbell Movement." With no intent at divisiveness, however, most of Campbell's followers continued calling themselves "Disciples of Christ" or "Christians." As the years passed, Campbell became increasingly critical of all the Protestant denominations, and was positively polemic about the Roman Catholic Church. In 1837 he engaged in an eight-day debate with the cardinal-archbishop of Cincinnati. There is no record that this had any lasting effect on either side, although it aroused much interest at the time. The movement continued to grow, and today has about a million members in some four thousand congregations. Campbell died in 1866 at Bethany, West Virginia, where he had established a seminary, of which he had been the president for twenty-six years. A prolific writer, he left over sixty volumes of his writings.

In the middle of the nineteenth century a few congregations began to break away from the Stone-Campbell Movement. They called themselves the Churches of Christ, although they were not officially recognized as a separate religious body by the U.S. Bureau of the Census until 1906. The main reason it took so long is that the individual congregations had no central organization or collaboration with each other; this practice was followed because there is no indication in the New Testament of organization beyond the local congregation. While the congregations are surprisingly uniform in beliefs and practices, each is totally autonomous. Churches of Christ congregations are found in all fifty states, although their strongest representation is in the South. In the 1990s the U.S. Census recorded a membership of 1.7 million in thirteen thousand independent congregations. The Disciples of Christ church considers them to be part of the Stone-Campbell Movement, but they deny this association, claiming their origin to be the first-century church. Their (unofficial) web page states, "We are not Campbellites, but Christians only!"

In 1968 a representative meeting in Kansas City approved the uniting of all congregations of the Stone-Campbell Movement, accepting the name "The Christian Church (Disciples of Christ)," thus incorporating the names of both original groups, Stone's and Campbell's. The Churches of Christ were welcome at this meeting, but not seeing themselves as part of the movement, they declined to participate. Several congregations of the Stone-Campbell Movement also refused to participate, designating themselves "The Undenominational Fellowship of Christian Churches and Churches of Christ." Their objection was that since none of the first-century churches formed organizations, neither should they. Although they forsook any idea of organizing themselves, they recognized a fellowship based on their common beliefs. They object to the ecumenical activities of the newly unified Christian Church, but they also disagree with the Churches of Christ in their ban of anything not directly authorized in the New Testament (such as the use of musical instruments in worship).

Beliefs and Customs

It is difficult to make a statement about the beliefs and customs of this movement, because it is neither creedal nor confessional — members resist any attempt to define their faith by creeds or statements of faith. They aver that their only head is Jesus Christ and their only creed the Holy Bible. One of their spokesmen, Dr. Kenneth Teegarden, has written, "A person who is comfortable with a dogmatic approach would be disappointed in the Christian Church."[1]

One major difference that separates the Churches of Christ from the rest of the movement is that they accept in their worship and faith only what is explicitly stated in the Bible. Their statement is, "Where the Bible speaks, we speak; where it is silent, we are silent." Since the New Testament makes no mention of the use of candles, incense, or musical instruments in worship, these are rejected. The Disciples of Christ, on the other hand, forbid only what is explicitly or implicitly forbidden by the New Testament. They thus have no objection to the use of musical instruments, candles, and similar traditional accouterments of worship, although not all use them.

The practices of the Christian Churches are actually quite eclectic, in keeping with Thomas Campbell's early dream of an undenominational unified Christian Church. What Dr. Teegarden wrote of the Disciples is also true of the Churches of Christ:

1. Kenneth Teegarden, *We Call Ourselves Disciples* (Saint Louis: Bethany Press, 1983).

We Disciples have beliefs and practices in common with all sorts of Christians. These apparent similarities sometimes are superficial, sometimes fundamental. We baptize by immersion, so we look like Baptists. We have Communion every Sunday, so we look a bit like Roman Catholics. We stress the ministry of the laity, so we look a little like Quakers. Our congregations call their pastors rather than accepting assigned ministers, so in that respect we look like Presbyterians. We rely heavily on preaching and teaching, so we look somewhat like Methodists. We have a congregational government, so we look a lot like the United Church of Christ.[2]

The movement is uniform in its view of baptism and Communion. Baptism is only for believers (thus there is no infant baptism), and only by immersion. There is no formal statement as to whether baptism generates an indelible spiritual change in the believer (as is the belief of most of the mainstream Christian churches) or is simply a symbolic act of affirmation of faith (as the Baptists believe). It would appear from their writings that beliefs on the meaning of baptism are a matter of individual faith. Infants are dedicated to Christ, but this is not tantamount to baptism. It is simply an affirmation of the parents' commitment to raise the child in the Christian faith. The Disciples recognize the baptism of any other denomination (even infant baptism), but encourage a previously baptized person to reaffirm his faith in Christ before the congregation. The Churches of Christ vary in this — some do as the Disciples, some require re-baptism only of those baptized as infants, and some expect re-baptism of anyone not baptized as a believer and by immersion.

Communion, which they call the Lord's Supper, is a basic part of the worship of the Christian Churches — so much so that the logo of the Disciples of Christ is a chalice with the cross superimposed on it. While most Protestant churches celebrate Communion only monthly or quarterly, the Christian Churches celebrate it every Sunday. They base this on Acts 2:42[3] and Acts 20:7,[4] the same passages which have

2. Teegarden, *We Call Ourselves Disciples*.
3. "They devoted themselves to the apostles' teaching and to the fellowship, to the breaking of bread and to prayer" (NIV).
4. "On the first day of the week we came together to break bread. Paul spoke to the people" (NIV).

led the Catholic churches to celebrate weekly Communion. They also interpret these passages (as do the Catholic churches) to imply that the gospel should be preached every time Communion is celebrated. There is no stated theology about the presence of Christ in Communion. It would appear that some believe in the real presence (the objective presence of the resurrected Christ under the elements of bread and wine), while others are receptionist (believing that Christ's presence is a function of the faith of the believer). Most of the Christian Churches use wine for communion, although some Churches of Christ use unfermented grape juice.

There are no ordained clergy in the Christian Churches. The individual congregation chooses lay elders who have demonstrated piety and knowledge. These elders preach, preside at the Lord's Supper, and minister to the pastoral needs of the congregation. Since many congregations do not have any members who feel qualified to take on this responsibility, pastors are often called from outside the congregation. They are viewed, however, as trained peers, not as authority figures. Most do not use titles such as "the Reverend." While many are graduates of seminaries or similar institutions, this is not required for their selection. Pastors of smaller congregations often support themselves by secular jobs.

The original people that formed the Christian Churches blended frontier hardiness and pragmatism with a simple, direct biblical faith that led them to reject all the ceremonial trappings and theological complexity that had developed through eighteen centuries of Christianity. Stone's and Campbell's dream of Christian unity remains unrealized. The sincerity of their faith cannot be challenged, however, and is reflected in that of their followers today.

THE UNITED CHURCH OF CHRIST

Of the three major systems of ecclesiastical polity, the least restrictive is congregationalism.[1] As the name implies, it is completely nonhierarchical, giving each individual congregation full autonomy over its own doctrine, practice, and property. This polity applies to many groups other than those that use the term "congregational" in their names, including the Baptists, the Church of God, the Church of Christ, and the Campbellite denominations such as the Disciples of Christ. The name "congregational" is usually associated with the churches that descended directly from the seventeenth-century English Puritans, among whom were the so-called "Pilgrims" who settled in New England.[2] In 1957 there was a union that climaxed ecumenical efforts of several decades, uniting four of the traditional congregational churches to form the United Church of Christ (UCC). These were the Congregational Church (descendants of the New England Puritans); a large portion of the Christian Church (the "Campbellites"); and both the Evangelical Synod of North America (an originally Calvinist-Lutheran German-American church) and the Reformed Church in the United

1. The other two systems are episcopalianism, which is governed by the three-fold ministry of bishops, priests, and deacons; and presbyterianism, a form of government based on cooperative equal authority of "pastors" (ordained clergy) and "elders" (elected laity).

2. They were not on a pilgrimage, but were in self-imposed exile in order to escape persecution by the Church of England. Their dream of creating a holy nation, a "City of God," later caused them to be called "Pilgrims."

States[3] (an evangelical group founded in Pennsylvania in the nineteenth century by German-speaking Swiss Calvinists).

History

The origins of Congregationalism can be traced back as far as 1582, when an apostate Anglican priest, Robert Browne, argued that the Church of England was so corrupt that it should be considered "separated from the Body of Christ." He taught that all true Christians should refuse to acknowledge it as a Christian church and should form their own autonomous churches. His followers came to be known as Separatists.[4] At first they acknowledged as Christian only those who could give satisfactory evidence of a personal conversion and knowledge of Christ, and membership was accepted by vote of the congregation.[5] The congregation was fully autonomous, electing its members and its leaders, and having full authority to exercise discipline on both. Each congregation drew up a membership agreement called a covenant. The theology of these groups was strongly Calvinistic. While congregations were independent and totally autonomous, they recognized the importance of a close cooperation. They formed associations for mutual support, but with no congregation or individual having authority over any other. An essential teaching to them was the separation of church and state. This meant that the church must have absolutely no authority in the state, and vice versa — each was to mind its own business and not interfere with the other. In the early New England settlements, however, for all practical purposes, the church and the state

---

3. The Evangelical Synod of North America and the Reformed Church in the United States had already merged in 1934. See the chapter on the Reformed churches for more information.

4. Another group, known as the Non-Separatists, did not deny the validity of the Anglican Church, but they disagreed with its teachings, sympathizing with the doctrines of the Separatists. They simply wanted the right to worship in their own way, free from any authority of the Church of England. Most of the settlers in Boston and Salem were Non-Separatists, while those in Plymouth were Separatists.

5. This doctrine was later eased; those who clung to it assiduously eventually broke away and formed the Baptist movement.

were one. In effect, these settlements were theocracies.[6] As they grew and matured, the doctrine of separation of church and state came more and more into practice. The Congregationalists' interpretation of it, however, was that neither should have authority over the other, not that the state should be protected from religion.

The original concepts of Congregationalism were based on the total sharing of work and goods, and on total equality of rank and power among members. Their social structure was pure communalism.[7] The Anglicans and Presbyterians argued that "independency" could only lead to civil and religious chaos. The American Puritans, in an attempt to refute them, sought to develop an exemplary, orderly, God-centered communalist community "without pope, prelate, presbytery, prince, or parliament." The governor presided over a community of his equals, and wealth and authority were to be equally distributed. The Plimoth (Plymouth) Plantation in Massachusetts soon discovered that untrammeled human nature inevitably overcame Christian intentions, and that communalism was doomed to fail. They therefore instituted a regulated capitalist system under which people could own property and keep a portion of the returns of their work, and the community began to prosper.

It must also be pointed out that the tale that the Puritans came to New England to establish religious freedom is a myth; they came only for their own religious freedom. Any deviation from the community's interpretation of the gospel was dealt with severely, with punishments ranging from public humiliation and scourging to exile, mutilation, and death. The Connecticut Puritans were somewhat more tolerant of those who disagreed with them, although they severely persecuted

6. Thus it was that in 1692 the church in Salem, Massachusetts, having the right to discipline its own members, also had legal authority to search out, try, and execute "witches." The cooperation of autonomous churches was also evident in this debacle. The minister from Beverly helped the Salem church in the early investigations, and later Cotton Mather came from Boston to help quell the madness that had finally exploded in Salem.

7. This simply means that there was to be no ownership of property, all decision-making was to be done with equal voice and vote of the community, and all community resources were to be equally shared. It should not be confused with the more restricted political-economic theory of Communism as defined by Marx and corrupted by Lenin and Mao.

Roman Catholics, Quakers, Jews, and atheists. In England, Puritans were treated as cruelly as they treated others in America. Attempts by the Church of England to stamp out nonconformity simply fueled the fires, with the final result being the English Civil War. In Parliament, Cromwell paved the way for the Congregationalists. They gained strong acceptance by the majority, the Presbyterians, who saw them as brothers in persecution under Charles I Stuart and the Church of England.

As is often the case with churches, the Congregational churches were at their best during their persecution. After Cromwell's victory, when the pressure was off, they quickly succumbed to the influences of rationalism, convenience, and materialism. After the Restoration, many congregations, weary of the dour austerity of Puritanism, returned to Anglicanism. By the end of the eighteenth century, many congregations, both in England and in America, had become Unitarian or simply had broken up and disappeared. In 1833 the surviving individual congregations recognized the need for mutual help and support and founded the Congregational Union of England and Wales. This provided for a centralized association, with an annual meeting and a president who should serve a one-year term. They defined their common beliefs, and in 1871 published a "Declaration of the Faith, Church Order, and Discipline of the Congregational or Independent Dissenters."

American Congregationalism became organized in the early eighteenth century with the formation of loosely defined regional associations. While in theory each congregation is totally autonomous, it is not quite so in practice. No minister is recognized as such without the approval of the association to which his congregation belongs. Also, there are strict rules governing the behavior and general teachings of ministers and congregations. A violation of these standards can result in expulsion from the association and a revocation of the right to use the title "Congregational." This is actually the result of something of a compromise made when the four churches merged. The Congregational and Christian Churches were congregational in polity, while the Evangelical Synod and Reformed Churches were presbyterian.

Most UCC congregations have deacons, but they vary greatly in their view of this role. Deacons are not considered clergy as they are in the Catholic churches, although some congregations see them as assistants to the clergy and give them the title of deacon for life. Others see them more as lay leaders of the congregation, much like vestrymen in the Episcopal Church. Still others see them in a nurturing servant role, and have them visit the sick and prisoners, care for shut-ins, and the like.

Beliefs

The UCC is a "covenantal" church. This means that while as a body it embraces certain beliefs and values, it has no hierarchical authority to impose these beliefs on individual members or on member congregations. The goal is to find a balance between individual conscience and traditional apostolic faith. The church is clearly Trinitarian, recognizing Jesus Christ as the head of the church. It accepts a large number of classic Christian documents, including the Apostles' and Nicene Creeds, Luther's *Small Catechism,* the *Heidelberg Catechism,* and the *Barmen Declaration.*[8] There is also a "Statement of Faith" that reads much like a contemporary creed. The UCC is not bound by any of these teachings, however — it looks to them as "testimonies, but not tests of the faith."

The UCC accepts the two sacraments commanded by Jesus, baptism and Holy Communion. Baptism may be administered by any of the three traditional methods, aspersion (sprinkling water), affusion (pouring water), or immersion in water. The most common method by far is affusion. Communion is usually administered monthly (the tradition is the first Sunday of the month), although individual congregations vary from quarterly to weekly. Wine may be used, but most congregations use unfermented grape juice. Theological interpretations vary greatly. Some accept a Calvinist view of the real presence of Christ in the Sacrament (dependent upon the faith of the believer). Others see Communion as a ritual memorial or reenactment of Christ's sacrifice. The moral and theological position of the UCC is clearly

8. This was a 1934 statement drawn up at Barmen by a group led by Karl Barth (Reformed) and Hans Asmussen (Lutheran). It repudiates the pressure from the Nazi government to "Aryanize" Europe and accept "the Führer Principle" as the guiding principle of European Christian churches. It declares that authority in the church lies exclusively with Jesus Christ.

stated in a 1993 document, "Toward the 21st Century: a Statement of Commitment." In this they affirm that they will be "a Church attentive to the Word," listening for God's guidance and revelation, and "a Church inclusive of all people," encouraging and seeking the diversity of God's creation. They further dedicate themselves to be "a Church responsive to God's call" and "a Church supportive of one another."

The faith of the member congregations of the UCC is well summed up in the preamble to the Constitution of the UCC: "The United Church of Christ acknowledges as its sole head, Jesus Christ, Son of God and Savior. It acknowledges as kindred in Christ all who share in this confession. It looks to the Word of God in the Scriptures, and to the presence and power of the Holy Spirit, to prosper its creative and redemptive work in the world. It claims as its own the faith of the historic Church expressed in the ancient creeds and reclaimed in the basic insights of the Protestant Reformers. It affirms the responsibility of the Church in each generation to make this faith its own in reality of worship, in honesty of thought and expression, and in purity of heart before God. In accordance with the teaching of our Lord and the practice prevailing among evangelical Christians, it recognizes two sacraments: Baptism and the Lord's Supper or Holy Communion."

THE HOLINESS AND
PENTECOSTAL MOVEMENTS

While Pentecostal experiences have been found in Christianity since apostolic times, the Holiness and Pentecostal movements in America are much more recent, having emerged in the nineteenth and twentieth centuries. Pentecostalism is characterized by a post-conversion charismatic[1] religious experience, usually called "Baptism in the Holy Spirit." This is indicated by glossolalia, "speaking in tongues," which is speaking in an unknown language alleged to be divine. This experience is often accompanied by physical events such as screaming, trembling, gyrating, or falling as if in an epileptic seizure.[2] It is a reflection of the experience of the apostles on the Day of Pentecost as recorded in Acts 2:1-13, when fire descended upon the apostles' heads and they spoke in tongues.

The Holiness Movement

Preceding the rise of Pentecostalism in America was the Holiness Movement, which is rooted in the teachings of John Wesley, the founder

1. The term "charismatic" refers to a personal religious experience involving divinely given powers such as prophecy, healing, and speaking or interpreting divine languages (tongues). It comes from a Greek word meaning "divine favor."

2. Because of these signs detractors sometimes refer to Pentecostals as "Glicky-glucks" (alluding to speaking with tongues) or "Holy Rollers" (alluding to the physical experiences). These terms are pejorative and offensive.

of Methodism. Wesley challenged all Christians to strive for perfection. He argued that the God who is good enough to forgive sins and save mankind is also powerful enough to sanctify mankind — in other words, to make sinners into saints. Perfection, he said, would free us from all sin and temptation, thus imbuing us with holiness. American Methodism's stated purpose in the early days was "to spread Christian holiness over these lands." In practice, however, the doctrine of perfection was paid little attention by early nineteenth-century Methodists. In 1843 about two dozen Methodist ministers renounced the Methodist Episcopal Church.[3] Designating themselves "Holiness Ministers," they founded the Wesleyan Methodist Church of America, with a strong focus on the doctrine of perfection and on the inspiration of the Holy Spirit. This set the pattern for a large number of smaller schisms and defections in all the Protestant churches. The Holiness Movement, as it came to be called, attracted huge numbers of Protestants from the rural Midwest and South. Many adopted puritanical codes of discipline and dress and openly disdained the traditional churches, which they associated with wealth, power, and religious formality.

Between 1880 and 1915 a large number of Holiness groups developed, some out of religious fervor, some to meet local social needs, and some simply to protest the dull routine into which most of the established churches seemed to have fallen. Many faded into obscurity, but a few grew strong and are still powerful voices in Protestantism today. Among them are the Church of God, the Christian and Missionary Alliance, the Free Methodist Church, the Church of the Nazarene, and the Salvation Army, all of which are now worldwide movements. The Church of the Nazarene is the largest group in the Holiness Movement, representing about a third of its members.

The Holiness churches have severed sufficient ties with their Methodist beginnings that they are today considered a separate Protestant group. They are fundamentalist and accept the Bible as having been literally dictated by God, and, of course, as being the sole source of Christian doctrine. They look for the second coming of Christ, particularly as described in the book of Revelation. They prac-

---

3. As was pointed out in the chapter on Methodism, this group was unrelated to the Episcopal Church. The name simply indicated their form of hierarchical church administration.

tice baptism (usually by immersion, and never of infants) and celebrate Communion. Baptism and Communion are practiced because
Christ commanded them, not because the Holiness churches attribute
a sacramental significance to these acts as the Catholic and mainline
Protestant churches do. Many Holiness churches have some charismatic practices, but they do not, for the most part, consider themselves
Pentecostal. In fact, many strongly disapprove of Pentecostalism.

Pentecostalism

Pentecostalism rose out of the Holiness Movement. Pentecostals hold
most of the same values and customs as the Holiness churches, with
the addition of the charismatic emphasis — the belief that with the
baptism in the Holy Spirit the individual will speak in tongues and receive at least one of the gifts of the Holy Spirit: interpreting tongues,
prophecy, or healing. Their regular services frequently contain these
elements. Although all Pentecostals share very similar beliefs, they
have not united into a single group.

Pentecostalism as it is known today began on the first day of the
twentieth century. Charles F. Parham, a Holiness minister and the di-
rector of the Bethel Bible Institute of Topeka, Kansas, often preached
that the staid, formalistic church of his time could only be revived by a
new infusion of the Holy Spirit. He admonished his students, most of
whom were of Methodist or Holiness backgrounds, to pray for such an
event and to prepare themselves spiritually for its coming. On January
1, 1901, one of his students experienced a "Spirit baptism," speaking in
an unknown tongue. Thereafter glossolalia became accepted as adequate evidence of baptism in the Holy Spirit. Since they identified this
experience with that of the giving of the Holy Spirit on Pentecost, they
began to call themselves Pentecostals. The experience spread, convincing most of the followers of this new movement that the second coming of Christ must be at hand. This gave them a sense of urgency to
evangelize the American southwest before the end of the world. Their
work was so successful that by 1905 there were more than twenty-five
thousand Pentecostals in Texas alone. The burst of growth was regional, however, covering only Kansas, Missouri, Texas, Alabama, and
northwestern Florida.

Often spiritual explosions come from the most unlikely sources. In Houston, Texas, Parham converted a rural Holiness preacher, an uneducated and nearly blind black man named William Seymour. He moved to Los Angeles and established the Apostolic Faith Gospel Mission on Azusa Street. From early 1906 on, the old wooden building became a focus of pilgrimages from all over the world. People of all races and social classes flocked to Azusa Street for spiritual guidance. Inspired with new evangelistic fervor they returned to their homes and started tabernacles and storefront missions all over the world, from which the Pentecostal movement flourished.

At first, Pentecostals did not see themselves as members of a new movement, let alone a new Protestant denomination. Most of them returned to their own churches where they continued practicing glossolalia, prophecy, and healing, in hope of infusing a revival of spiritual energy into their own denominations. They believed that the Holy Spirit would cause the "latter rain" of spiritual truth to fall generously on all Christianity. What they met, of course, was opposition and occasionally outright persecution. Pastors who embraced Pentecostalism were expelled from their pulpits, and lay people were ostracized or forcibly ejected from their churches. Even as outcasts, however, Pentecostals resisted any kind of organization. They feared the encroachment of external authority and worried that the same problems they had seen previously in the organized denominations would arise in their own churches.

The unfortunate result of this lack of organization was the growth of a heterogeneity that threatened to make them completely ineffective as evangelists. Many self-anointed preachers preyed on congregations that could not distinguish the wolves in sheep's clothing. There was no check on finances, thus inviting corruption and theft. Several leaders, recognizing that the dangers of organization were far surpassed by the evils that were emerging in the movement, attempted to establish unity and form a recognizable Pentecostal denomination. They were unsuccessful, however, and to this day Pentecostal congregations range from the fully charismatic and spontaneous to the organized, ritualistic, and hierarchical. They also range from those that have formed local or regional organizations to the hundreds of storefront churches that defy classification. They can be found in sophisticated urban areas and in remote rural and mountain regions. It is in the latter that the more extreme physical and emotional manifestations are most often found. Some Pentecostal churches have organized on a worldwide basis, the largest being the Assemblies of God, the Church of God in Christ, the Church of God, and the United Pentecostal Church International.

One of the reasons people found Pentecostalism so appealing is that as the traditional churches became more firmly established in America in the latter part of the nineteenth century, many of them became wealthy and influential and seemed to be interested in ministering only to "socially acceptable" people.[4] This made the lower and poorer classes feel left out, and they sought a religious expression that they felt was more sympathetic to their needs. While Pentecostalism ministers to all classes and races, by far its greatest numbers are among the economically, educationally, and socially deprived.

Another of the great appeals of Pentecostalism is the phenomenon of spiritual healing, predicated on the biblical teaching that Christ will heal the sick if they have sufficient faith. While the traditional churches for the most part also believe in and practice faith healing, it is usually done in a formal, liturgical, and dignified manner. Also, in most cases it is not high on their list of priorities. In contrast, many Pentecostals practice faith healing accompanied by much emotionalism — shouting alleluias, prayers, and commands to be healed, and often literally pushing or knocking the subject to the floor. This dramatic approach seems to appeal to at least as many people as it offends. Among the most famous Pentecostal preacher-healers are Aimee Semple McPherson, Oral Roberts, and Jimmy Lee Swaggart.

On October 4, 1997, the largest religious assembly in American history took place on the Mall in Washington, D.C., when 1.5 million men gathered at the first rally of the Promise Keepers. This group crosses all denominations, but its founder, Bill McCartney, comes from the charismatic tradition, as do by far the largest portion of its members. A week earlier the world conference of the Assemblies of God took place in São Paulo, Brazil, with more than a million men and women attending. In 1995 there were 43,582 Pentecostal churches rep-

---

4. This is, in fact, a sad commentary on the failure of many churches to meet St. Paul's admonition to be "all things to all people."

resenting over 10 million members,[5] plus thousands of small independent tabernacles and storefront churches which are almost impossible
to tally.

Pentecostal educational institutions are also booming. In 1997 Pat
Robertson sold his TV company, the Family Channel, and gave $150
million of the profits to Regent University in Virginia, making it the
best endowed evangelical university in the world. Pentecostal colleges
and universities all across the country are growing at an astounding
rate. In 1997 the Assemblies of God Theological Seminary dedicated its
new $4.5 million building debt free.

Many independent Pentecostal churches are moving closer to
uniting with existing organizations, and several mergers among Pentecostal organizations have taken place in the past few years. It appears that the organizational dreams of a few visionary leaders in the
early part of the century are finally coming to pass.

5. 1995 Yearbook of the National Council of Churches of Christ in the USA.

THE ADVENTISTS

The Adventist Movement represents a number of worldwide Protestant denominations that are all distinguished by an expectation of the imminent return of Christ to the world — the Second Coming. They believe that this return, or Advent, will be a personal, visible return of Christ in glory, at which time the righteous will be separated from the wicked, and the one-thousand-year reign of Christ (the millennium) will begin. To Americans, the best known of these Adventist denominations is the Seventh Day Adventist Church.

Beliefs and Customs

Most (though not all) of the fundamental beliefs of the Adventists are shared with many Protestant churches. They include the following: The Holy Scriptures are the written Word of God, divinely inspired and infallible. There is one God in three persons (the Holy Trinity), Father, Son, and Holy Spirit. Christ's life, death, and resurrection atoned for man's sin in obedience to the will of God, providing forgiveness of sins and ultimate victory over death. The church is the community of believers who confess Jesus Christ as Lord and Savior, and is continuous with and a fulfillment of the Old Testament. Baptism is a testimony of the faith of the believer, and is only by immersion. Communion is a reenactment and commemoration of the Last Supper, in remembrance of Christ's proclamation of his death at that time. It is

182

open to all believing Christians and is always accompanied by foot-washing. Marriage is a lifelong bond in which the commitments to God and to the spouse are equal. It is indissoluble except, as Jesus allowed, for adultery.

In the above beliefs, the Adventists are not unlike the Baptists. They distinguish themselves, however, in several ways. Most Adventists, and especially the Seventh Day Adventist Church, adhere to the Old Testament command to honor the seventh day (Saturday) as the Sabbath. It is observed from sundown to sundown. They believe that God's commandment supercedes any human observance, even recognition of the resurrection, important as that is to them. Most other Christians observe Sunday as the Sabbath, since that is the day on which Christ arose.

Based on the scriptural teaching that the body is the temple of the Holy Spirit, Adventists abstain from eating meat, and they forbid the use of drugs or stimulants. They are not opposed to medical treatment, however. In fact, they maintain more than 360 hospitals and clinics around the world. They also support a huge network of philanthropic and educational programs, supported by the tithes of their members.[1] They publish a great variety of literature, including a well-prepared magazine, *Ministry,* which is sent free to any Christian clergyman who wishes to receive it, regardless of denomination. The Adventist parochial school system is second in size only to that of the Roman Catholic Church.

Adventists believe in the gift of prophecy as a manifestation of the "remnant church," the body of those who remain faithful to Christ to the end. All Adventists believe that their founder, William Miller, was a prophet. The Seventh Day Adventists also accept the prophetic gift of one of Miller's disciples, Ellen G. White.

While most Christians believe in the second coming of Christ, the Adventists put a particularly strong emphasis on it. When Christ comes, they believe, the righteous dead will rise, and they and the righteous living will be taken up into heaven; the wicked will die eternally. They also believe that this event is near at hand. Some attempt to interpret Scripture to determine an exact date. Most agree, however,

---

1. Since the Bible requires tithing (giving of 10 percent of one's income), all Adventists are expected to tithe.

that as Jesus said, it is not given for us to know when it will happen, so we must always be prepared.

Another belief that is emphasized far more heavily than in any other Christian group is that of the Great Controversy.[2] According to this concept, all humanity is involved in a great controversy between Satan and God. This began when Lucifer defied God, leading an army of angels in rebellion. He corrupted mankind and all creation when he involved Adam and Eve in sin. Mankind, which retains the distorted image of God, is ambivalent in its loyalty, being attracted to both good and evil. Ultimately God will be vindicated, and Christ sends the Holy Spirit to inspire us to ally with God, and the loyal angels to assist us.

There is one teaching that is unique to the Adventists. This is a belief that there is a heavenly sanctuary in which Christ ministers on our behalf. He has made his atoning action known to believers, even though we are not capable of fully understanding it. At his ascension he was inaugurated our Great High Priest, and began his intercessory ministry for us then. In 1844, at the end of a prophetic period of 2300 days, Christ entered the second and final phase of his atoning ministry. This phase is an investigatory judgment, determining who among the dead are righteous ("dead in Christ") and thus worthy to be resurrected at the final judgment. When Christ has completed this ministry he will return to earth.

When Christ returns, the Adventists believe, the righteous living and dead will be transported to heaven, where Christ will rule for one thousand years. During this time the earth will be desolate, with no human inhabitants. Satan and his minions will live on earth. At the end of the millennium Christ and the Holy City will be transported back to earth. The unrighteous dead will be resurrected, and they, with Satan and the evil spirits, will be consumed by heavenly fire. The earth will be purified, and will become the eternal home of all the righteous, with whom God will reside. The Great Controversy will be ended, and there will be no more sin, suffering, or death in the universe for all eternity.

2. This concept of the Great Controversy has distinctly Zoroastrian overtones. Zarathushtra taught that the righteous god, Ahura Mazda, is in conflict with the evil god, Ahriman, and that there will be a final conflict in which Ahriman is vanquished. This teaching entered Judaism during the Exile, and from there it became well ingrained in Christianity. Much of the prophecy of Armageddon is based on this.

History

The Adventist Movement began in the early nineteenth century during a period when many Protestant churches were experiencing a surge of interest in the millennium as described in the book of Revelation. One of the primary founders of the movement was William Miller (1782-1849). As an Army officer in the War of 1812, Miller, who had been raised a Baptist, began to lose his faith. He devoted himself to a study of the Bible, was converted back to belief, and began to preach as a Baptist. During his study he had been particularly fascinated by the books of Daniel and Revelation, both of which focus heavily on the Great Controversy and the end of all things. He concluded that the Second Coming would take place sometime between the vernal equinoxes of 1833 and 1844. When this period passed without event, he corrected his calculations and announced that it would take place on October 22, 1844. This day also passed uneventfully, and came to be known as the "Great Disappointment." Miller's followers, called "Millerites" by the press, concluded that the date had been right, but that they had misinterpreted the event. They argued on the basis of Daniel 8 and 9 that the "cleansing of the heavenly sanctuary" had begun. This meant that Christ had begun an examination of all the names in the Book of Life, judging who is righteous and who is wicked. When this task was completed, he would return. During the ensuing years one of Miller's early disciples, Ellen White, developed into a gifted author, speaker, and administrator, and was an important figure in the growth of the church. She came to be accepted by most Adventists as having prophetic authority and a special relationship with God, and many still consider her a prophetic figure. After Miller's death in 1849 she became the *de facto* leader of the movement.

In 1863 the Millerites founded the Seventh Day Adventist Church, based on the teachings of William Miller. This is the largest of the Adventist bodies, and is the main one that observes the Sabbath on Saturday, the day of the Jewish Sabbath. Other groups also soon emerged, based on Miller's teachings. These include the Advent Christian Church and the several branches of the Church of God. They all observe the Sabbath on Sunday, and reject the dietary laws. There are some variations in emphasis and focus among these groups, but in general they follow Miller's original teachings. Most, however, reject Ellen White's status as a prophet. They are congregational in polity, as are all Adventist groups. An ultra-conservative group, the Primitive Advent Church, has recently formed in West Virginia. It is dedicated to the restoration of the principles and thought of the earliest days of Adventism. It is a very small group, but it is growing rapidly.

In 1874 the Seventh Day Adventists sent out their first missionary, John Nevins Andrews, who worked mainly in Latin America. The church soon spread to the Caribbean and sub-Saharan Africa, and to a small degree into Europe. Today it has over 750,000 members in the United States, and almost 10 million members worldwide. It is by far the largest of the several Adventist churches.

Many mainstream Protestants tend to dismiss the Adventists as an insignificant "sect" within Christianity. This is a distinct mistake. Although a relatively new arrival on the timeline of church history, the Adventist Movement has a very significant following, and is having an increasingly profound influence on conservative Protestantism around the world.

THE CHRISTIAN SCIENTISTS

The Church of Christ, Scientist, while one of the smaller denominations, had a significant impact on twentieth-century Protestantism. In the latter part of the nineteenth century Christianity was torn between what Mary Baker Eddy, the founder of the Christian Science church, called "stern Protestantism" and "doubtful liberalism." During that era, the search of many Christians for something new and different led to the rise of a number of movements that diverged from traditional mainstream Christianity. The most notable were the Adventists, the Holiness Movement, and their offshoot, the Pentecostals. Some searchers went even further afield and settled on pseudo-Christian groups such as the Jehovah's Witnesses. It was in this atmosphere of spiritual searching that Christian Science was conceived.

History

Mary Baker was born in 1821 in Bow, New Hampshire. Her parents were devout but inflexibly Calvinist Congregationalists. At an early age she rebelled against her parents' harsh puritanism, although she resisted the temptation to turn to the other extreme of Unitarianism, a popular religion at the time. Her health was frail and she had a severe spinal malady, so her education was limited and often interrupted, although she received extensive tutoring at home from her brother Albert. In 1843 she married George Glover, who died before her only

187

child, also named George, was born. Because of her health she was not able to rear the child, and she had little contact with him. She began to explore the Bible more and more deeply in search of an answer to human suffering. She sought a number of alternative healing methods, including homeopathy[1] and herbs.

In 1853 she married Daniel Patterson, a dentist who shared this interest, but it was an unhappy union, and ended in divorce. In 1862 she met Phineas Parkhurst Quimby, a charismatic faith healer from Maine. While she ultimately rejected most of his teachings, he had a profound influence in convincing her that all disease is a function of the mind and spirit. Quimby approached healing from a psychological viewpoint, however, while she was convinced that it was the result of God's action on the human spirit. After Quimby's death in 1865 her illness returned. In 1866 she had a serious fall and was told that she would be a cripple for life. She turned to the New Testament for guidance, searching it in detail. Within a few months she had completely recovered and was free from pain. She regarded this as the beginning of Christian Science. She discussed her findings at length and began to take on disciples, some of whom became successful faith healers. In order to support herself she accepted students for a fee, and her fortunes took a substantial turn for the better. In 1875 she published *Science and Health,* which would be revised and expanded several times (the last time in 1910) as *Science and Health: with Key to the Scriptures.* This book clearly explained her faith and teachings and is believed by her followers to have been divinely inspired. It, along with the Bible, is considered the "textbook" of Christian Science. In 1877 Mary married Asa G. Eddy, one of her disciples.

In 1879 Mary Baker Eddy and fifteen of her followers founded the Church of Christ, Scientist, with the stated goal of returning to the principles of "primitive Christianity and its lost element of healing." In 1882 they moved their headquarters to Boston, and this began a long period of growth. There they established The Mother Church, which today is still the international headquarters of Christian Science.

---

1. Homeopathy is a nineteenth-century alternative system of medicine based on the idea that a disease can be cured by dosing the victim with tiny quantities of a substance that produces symptoms of the disease in a healthy person. Its goal is to remove the cause of the disease, not simply to eliminate its symptoms.

Its beautiful building at the side of a reflecting pool is one of Boston's important tourist sites. One of the main attractions of the Church of Christ, Scientist, was its success in healing work, carried on by students trained by Eddy. By 1890 there were over one hundred congregations, and by her death in 1910 there were over twelve hundred. The church continued to grow steadily until the time of World War II, but since then it has been slowly but consistently declining. In 1898 the church determined that it would not release membership figures, so current numbers are not available. According to the National Council of Churches census, however, there were twenty-four hundred Christian Science congregations in the United States in 1995.

Beliefs and Customs

Christian Science takes its name from the basic meaning of the term "science." Science is the systematic search for knowledge and the practical application of the principles discovered. Christian Science seeks to develop our knowledge of God by developing our relationship with him, and to apply that knowledge in order to attain spiritual and thus physical health. Jesus operated on the basis of divine principles, and is thus the ultimate Scientist. He, having revealed these principles to us, expects us to live by them. Christian Science accepts the traditional Christian belief in an omnipotent, personal, purposeful God who created all things. It accepts the Bible as God's revelation to man, but does not believe it to be literally inerrant. While the term Trinity rarely appears in their writings, Christian Scientists do believe in the three divine persons of God: Father, Son, and Holy Spirit. Their view of Christ is common to all Christians, that he is the Son of God, the Redeemer, and the Savior. They accept without challenge the gospel accounts of his virgin birth, life, death, resurrection, and ascension. Christian Science has been accused of denying the divinity of Christ, but there is no evidence in their literature to support this charge. There is no creed or formal statement of faith, although the body of their beliefs regarding God, Christ, the Holy Spirit, and the atonement are common with those of traditional Christianity. They do not accept heaven and hell as specific destinations after death, but as states of mind, experienced to varying degrees in this life as well as after death.

Christian Scientists observe no sacraments. They define baptism as commanded by Jesus to mean "the daily, ongoing purification of thought and deed." Communion with God is achieved with silent prayer and Christian living. Generally the only prayer that is said aloud is the Lord's Prayer. All other prayer is considered to be a personal and private communion with God. People pray together, but they do so silently. God is frequently referred to with the phrase, "God, good."

Christian Scientists believe that sin, suffering, disease, and death do not originate in God — God's will for mankind is pure good and pure love. Evil, which is real and a challenge to God's power, originates in man's false belief that he is separated from God. Since this belief is false, then sin and suffering are not true realities. All evils in the world can be vanquished simply by man's realization that they are not real. The goal of Christian Science is to help achieve that awareness. The church does not offer advice to members in any personal matters but only helps guide people to find answers through prayer. It teaches strict adherence to the Ten Commandments, the Sermon on the Mount, and all the other moral and social teachings of Jesus as recorded in the Bible. Trained "practitioners" are available to lead people through prayer to a solution to their personal problems, including physical and mental illness, marital difficulties, addiction, and abuse. Addictive or intoxicating drugs, tobacco, and stimulants are forbidden. There is no formal punishment for breaking that prohibition, but the church diligently teaches how their use itself punishes and enslaves the user.

Christian Science does not practice "faith healing" in the usual sense of the word. Faith healing as practiced by groups such as the Pentecostals requires that the patient have faith that God will heal him, or that the disease be caused by an evil spirit that can be expelled at the command of the healer. Christian Science, while it expects that the patient have faith, relies on an ever-increasing understanding of what it means to be one with God. This is achieved by prayer, not by "blind faith." Christian Science healing uses no incantations, secret writings, or "mind-over-matter" techniques. It is not an act of human will, but an act of learning to recognize God's will.

Christian Science has no clergy in the traditional sense. There are "practitioners," men and women who devote their full time to healing. To be a practitioner requires a deep devotion and a dedicated prayer life, as well as extensive study and a demonstrated ability to apply spiritual understanding to the overcoming of human ills. It also requires a formal course of study with an authorized teaching practitioner, and a record of success in healing. A practitioner is not a therapist or a counselor. He is a spiritual guide who works with the patient in his spiritual journey.

A common misconception about Christian Scientists is that they forbid medical treatment. While they believe that medical treatment is a man-made thing that ultimately is of no avail, any Christian Scientist is free to use medical services if he wishes, either as the sole treatment or in conjunction with prayer. This would not incur reproach or expulsion from the church. It would be rather pointless, of course, to be a Christian Scientist and rely at all heavily on medicine. Many, however, would accept the treatment of a surgeon to set a broken bone or suture a serious wound, and then rely on Christian Science for the subsequent healing. Christian Scientists also teach full adherence to the law. If the law requires, for example, they will call an attending physician or licensed midwife for childbirth, and they cooperate fully with mandated vaccination or quarantine programs. While they believe that such treatments are pointless, they also see them as harmless. There are trained Christian Science nurses. Their function is not medical, but nurturing — they bathe patients, comfort them, dress their wounds, and oversee their nutrition, among other things. Some work in the patients' homes, and others at Christian Science nursing facilities.

Christian Scientists, both as individuals and as congregations, do not hesitate to come to the aid of victims of poverty, social oppression, war, and natural disaster. They did extensive relief work during both world wars and are prepared to mobilize relief efforts in case of disasters. They have few formal relief programs in place, however, as they believe that such programs simply put a "Band-aid" on the problem without going to the root of it. The root of all evil, as was described above, is man's belief in his separation from God. The only treatment, therefore, is prayer, and they pray fervently for the law of love to be recognized and thus bring healing to the world.

Christian Science worship consists of congregational, choral, and solo singing, instrumental music (usually organ or piano), silent prayer, the Lord's Prayer said aloud, Bible readings, a sermon, and a collection. They observe Sunday as a holy day, as do most other Christians. In addition there is a Wednesday service that also includes readings from *Science and Health* and testimonies of healing from members of the congregation. All services are conducted by lay readers, and are open to the public.

The church is governed by the standards established by Mary Baker Eddy in 1910 in the *Church Manual* — its polity is congregational. The international business of the Mother Church is conducted by a board of directors. Each individual congregation is democratically governed as a "branch church" of the Mother Church. The local churches elect their own officers, and every member has an equal vote. They also elect delegates who elect the directors of the Mother Church.

A valuable contribution to the world at large is the publication of one of the world's leading newspapers, the Pulitzer Prize–winning *Christian Science Monitor*. One of its primary goals is to present unbiased reporting of world and national affairs while maintaining a constructive and healing point of view.

Scattered around the world, mainly in larger cities and towns, are Christian Science Reading Rooms. A Reading Room is a combination library, bookstore, and study room where the public has free access to Christian Science publications, including the *Monitor*, as well as Bibles and literature on scriptural interpretation. Members of the local congregation make themselves available to answer questions or teach about Christian Science.

Christian Science had an impact on twentieth-century Christianity that is well out of proportion to its size. It accepted total equality of men and women long before society or most of Christianity was ready to do so. Most Christian churches practice spiritual healing in one form or another, yet a huge number of documented "medically unexplainable" healings can be attributed to Christian Science. This unquestionably has been a major factor in reawakening an interest in spiritual healing in the mainstream church, as well as having spurred a fervid interest in it in the denominations and movements that arose in the nineteenth century, such as the Adventists and the Pentecostals.